War and Paracetam

OR

The Bic is Back!

AN OMNIBUS COMPRISING

The Cancer Collection

AND

The F***ing Scary Virus Diaries

by Bob Goody

Illustrations by SHEILA RUSKIN

This edition published by Bx3
an imprint of Burning Eye Books 2021

Burning Eye Books
15 West Hill, Portishead, BS20 6LG, United Kingdom

ISBN 978-1-913958-25-1

To Gina
The beautiful lady
That I love

Special thanks
to

SHEILA RUSKIN - *our wonderful illustrator*
HUW GWILLIAM - *our wonderful designer*
DOC LUKE DIXON - *our wonderful ringmaster*

THE CANCER COLLECTION

Woke Up One Morning

Woke up one morning
Feeling good
Took my pill for anxiety
Mug of Earl Grey tea
Plain choccy bic
Lovely
Went to the lavatory
Standard form of a morn
Sat down...stood up...
Found some blood
Where blood shouldn't be
Shit! I thought
Quite apt, in a way
My day very nearly
Dissolved
Caught myself in the mirror
I rallied
Probably a spot, I said
A sore bit, a rash
A nod of sympathy
From this bloke
Staring back at me
Decided to ignore it!

Next day...
I woke
Feeling...
Not so good
Took my pill for anxiety
Mug of Earl Grey tea
Passed on the choccy bic
(Wasn't hungry)
Nervously...
I went to the lavatory
Sat down...
Stood up...
No blood
NO BLOOD!

Did a semi-naked dance of joy
In a confined space
Pyjams round my knees
Fists waving, bollocks flying
It was a spot
A sore bit, a rash
It was!!
Phew! Fuck!

And on the third day...
I woke
Feeling...fine
Took my pill for anxiety
Tea, bic, lavatory
Sat down...
And rose up...
Blood!
Shit! (Apt)
BLOOD!
FUCK!
GP
Arse
Internal
Finger
Ouch!
Sorry
Something
A lump
Haemorrhoids?
Tumour?
Possibly
Shit! (Apt)
FUCK!
Hospital
Doctor (Registrar)
Arse
Internal
Finger

Ouch!
Sorry
Now...
Disposable gloves off!
Direct
No messing (Distressing)
Lump
Tumour
Bowel Cancer
(Probably)
Operation
Arse amputation
Shit
Will then
Be coming
Out of my tummy
Into a fucking bag
For fuck's sake!!
For the rest of my days
Then he said
(And here's the bad news!)
The cancer may have spread
To my lungs, my liver
I could be dead
Very soon, I thought
The end of life
Terrified
Numb
I took my wife
To the pub
For a calming beer
(Or several)
I'd always had a chronic fear
Of death
And the present situation

Was not exactly helping matters
CT Scan
MRI Scan
Colonoscopy
Arse...again
(But not for much longer!)
Internal
Camera
Ouch!
Sorry
Biopsy
Malignant
Life oh life
Please don't leave me!
Two weeks later
I was under the knife
(For five and a half hours)
Cut up
In a not dissimilar way
To how you might prepare
A chicken carcass
After the Sunday roast
For a heart-warming broth
When I came round
A little groggy, a little sore
I found
The tumour was no more
The cancer hadn't spread
I wasn't soon to be dead
I still had my life
And
I still had my wonderful wife
(And family)
(And friends)

Woke up one morning
Feeling...different
Took my pill for anxiety
Mug of peppermint tea
Plain choccy bic
Lovely
Went to the lavatory
Standard form of a morn
Caught myself in the mirror
Got a nod, and a smile
From this bloke staring back at me
Looked longingly at the toilet bowl
Had a sip of tea
Then...
I changed my colostomy bag

Cancer

Got cancer
(Of the bowel)
Thought I was
Going to die
Bit of a bugger
Upsetting
Was planting my chilli seedlings
On the patio
At the time
A yearly pursuit
Had a morbid thought
Won't be seeing
Those gleaming beautiful
Little arse burners
This year
Or any year...
Ever again!
Brought a tear
Very upsetting
Another thought...
May even, end up
Being scattered on said patio
In powdered form!
Another tear
Extremely upsetting
Or next year
Becoming fertilizer
In a decorative terracotta pot
Of chillies
On the patio
In memory
OF ME!
Fuck!

Even more upsetting
As it turned out
I didn't die
As you can see
(That line only works in a
Live reading, obviously!)
I just lost a few
Important bits
Of my body
(I was fond of)
That had been with me
For some years
Not quite so upsetting
But still
Not favourite

Am just harvesting my chillies
All red and green
And gleaming and glorious
Wafting in the autumn breeze
Will dry some
Will pickle some
May even munch some with Cheddar cheese
But one thing I can safely say
For sure
They won't be burning my arse
'Cos I don't have an arse
Anymore

The Night of The Turin Shroud
(A Hospital Experience)

Most of the nurses
Most of the time
Were
Mostly
Marvellous
But some of the nurses
Some of the time
Were
Sometimes
Horrid
I'd had my arse removed
Part of my bowel was missing
Had a stapled gash
From my balls
To my chest
And a bag of waste
Hung from my waist
So I wasn't best placed
To take on the curse
Of the uncaring nurse
Who
On seeing me
Convulsed with hiccups
Wracked with pain
A tummy extension fit for childbirth
Offered this wretched soul
A few sips of water
And a couple of paracetamol
Then...

On (coldly) handing me
A cardboard sick bowl
(Which, curiously I noticed
Resembled an upturned Trilby hat)
Said
By way of a parting blow
You're not the only person
Who's ever suffered from hiccups
You know
And left

The Lucky Ones

Got this magazine
Living with a colostomy
From Colostomy UK
Full of pictures
Of people
Who are
Incredibly happy
(I mean incredibly happy)
Frolicking through the surf
Romancing in the sand dunes
Gambolling through the dappled woods
All of whom
I assume
Are so incredibly happy
Because they have
A bag of shit
Hanging from their waist
In fact
They seem so much more
Incredibly happy
Than the majority of people
Who are
One could argue
Unlucky enough
Not to have
A bag of shit
Hanging from their waist
So I'm incredibly happy to say
I'm one of the lucky ones

Circles (Confusion)

Put my right boot
On my right foot
Put another right boot
From a different pair
Of boots
On my left foot
Thinking
I'd put the right boot
That being the left boot
From the first pair of boots
On my left foot
Found myself
Walking around
In circles
No changes there then

Got to Me

Totally overdid it yesterday
Found myself in a mental fog
Clogged up
All fears and welling tears
Hoped a pint of beer
Would clear it
So I could see
The wood for the trees
Sat in a crowded pub
Full of jolly local people
Opposite a very miserable man
Fucking Friday night, he said
I left
Leaving several mouthfuls
Of beer, behind
I never do that
Very worrying
Losing my mind
Things were no clearer
Had spent yesterday
And the day before
And the day before that
Writing a poem
About my penis
I think it got to me

Amazing

Came out of my flat
One night
There was the moon
A full moon
Rising
In the deep blue sky
At the end of the street
Just above the Highland Stores
Huge and crystal clear, it was
Nestling in amongst a few
Wispy white clouds
Stunning
Amazing
Felt compelled to share it
With a passer by
Look at that, I said
To the young lady
In the gabardine mac
What? she said
The moon, I said
The moon? she said
Yeah, the moon
It's just the moon, she said
I know, I said
But it's amazing eh?
It's just the moon, she said
And wandered on her way

Sunbeam

A tiny sunbeam
Through the clouds
On the water
Thought I oughta
Stop and marvel
So I sat on a bench
And marvelled
(Marvellous)
Then it was gone
Time to move on
But when I tried to rise
My knees
Had seized
Which I'm very pleased to say
Has absolutely nothing
To do
With cancer
I'm just getting old

First Night

It was my first night
Out
Three months on from when
The removal men
Took over my insides
I changed my colostomy bag
Donned a baggy lemon cotton shirt
A light linen suit
Jaunty Panama hat
And looking a tad tasty
I nervously
Set forth
I'd been invited to
The gala opening night
Of Fleabag
In London's glittering West End
Having made a less than brief
But meaningful appearance
In Series Two, Episode Four
Old man at Quaker meeting
The Wyndham's Theatre
The glitter
The glamour
The clamour of fans
Eager to catch a glimpse
Of Quaker Man!
I gave them a wave
A superior smile
Confidence soaring
I hit the Stalls Bar
Checked my bag
So far, no shit
Small glass of Pinot Noir
(Nice one)
Almost relaxed

I nodded to a few
Semi well known people
I sort of semi knew
They nodded back
With the expression
That said
Who the fuck are you?
The five minute bell
Off to the loo
No leakage
No caking
No ballooning (Phew!)
(Technical terms)
It was all going far too well
Me bum on me tum
Was behaving itself
Reminded me of the good times
When an arsehole was an arsehole
No messing
Ahh! Happy days...
The two minute bell
Snapped me out of my reverie
Off to the stalls
Row N, Seat 13
Unlucky for some
One or two excuse-mes
And I was settled
At ease
The cosy glow of the Pinot (Noir)
Now coursing through my head
For the first time
In a long time
It has to be said
I was in a state of relaxation
My mind, for once

Not consumed
With bags of shit
Around me
The bubble and babble of expectation
We waited...
The house faded to black
The audience faded to silence
Darkness
Happiness
A warm wash of light
On a single chair
(Silent anticipation)
Then...something
A feeling
I felt...a feeling
A rumble
Down below
A rumble, in my tumble
Oh no!
Rising...
Please!
Why won't the show begin?
The single chair
Empty!
Fleabag? Where the fuck are you?
Please!!
Then...
It came...
A strained, soggy, squelchy smelly sound
Which seemed to rebound
Off every wall
In every building
In the whole fucking world
Heads turned
Felt 949 pairs of eyes (approximately)

That's 1,998 eyes in total
Turning
Burning into my inner soul
I sat staring, rigid, sweating
Profusely
Willing the show to end
Even though it hadn't even begun

Fleabag was very very funny
But I didn't have much fun
I just sat, petrified, unsure
Expecting any second
My bag to return for an encore
Passed on the after show party
Thought, for safety
Mr Farty should head home
For a needy hug
With his darling wife Gina
And I decided
There and then
Never
To go out
Ever
Again
For the rest of my life

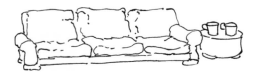

Soft Wipes

Soft wipes
My soft wipes
I can't find my soft wipes
I'm away from home
My first time
Since the operation
On my own
And consternation
I can't find my soft wipes!
Oh my God!
Fucking hell!
What will I do
If I have a shit
And I need the loo
(As it were)
And I have to change
My bag
Without my soft wipes!?
Fact is
I know I packed them (I know!)
Had a checklist, you see
Before I left
Made a tick
With my Bic
Stoma bags...tick
Removal spray...tick
Soft wipes...tick
In the mit, in the kit!
But they're not there!
They are not there!
Where the fuck are they?
I phone my wife in despair
Can't find my soft wipes darling, I say
Hello darling, says she
Calm as can be

Are you okay?
I'm fine, I say, I'm fine
It's just...my soft wipes...
I can't find my soft wipes
A moment
They're on the bed, she says
On the bed!? I say
On the bed, she says
On the BED!?
Yes Bob, she says, they're on the bed
No, no, no, no, no, I say
No they can't be
No way
That's insane
They cannot be on the bed
You are playing a game with me darling
I packed them
I know I packed them...NO!
Really, really darling
I remember soo clearly
I made a tick
With my Bic
Which you can't see, obviously
But please believe me
Then I put them in my bag changing kit...
Bag!
Absolutely definitely
A moment
Ah! I think I may, possibly be
Back in the race
Up to pace
After faltering in the middle laps
(Go on Nobby my son
There's only one winner!)
They're on the bed, she says

They're not! I bark
I hear
A little sigh
A gentle cry, maybe
A weary tear
Bobby, says she
What! I snap
As I said, they're on the bed
You packed an extra pack
Of waste bags instead
Aaaaagh!!
She's kicked for home
Left me for dead
I check my bag changing kit...bag
Fuck, fuck...and fuck!
She's right! She's right!
She's...right!
Shite!
And she's so fucking calm as well
It's a waking colostomy hell!!
Okay, okay, okay, you win, I say
You win
So...what do I do
What do I do NOW
If I have a shit
If I need the loo
How do I change my fucking bag
Without my soft wipes...
Eh!!??
Go to Boots, she says
Boots! I say
Go to Boots, she says
And buy some wipes
Ah! But darling, I say
Very good, very clever

However...however
I need the soft wipes, you see
The dry ones, the dry type
They only have the wet ones
The wet type
The wet wipes...in Boots
Silence
Ha haa!
A moment
I'm sensing there's still time
To pip her on the line
Bobby, she says
So calm...so ominous
What do you do
When you've had a poo
And you go to the loo? She says
Well, I say, I...lay out my kit
You lay out your kit
Then what do you do?
Bloody hell darling!
Is this necessary? I say
I think it is, she says
Okay, okay, I say, okay
I take my removal spray...
You take your removal spray...
Yes, and I remove my bag
You remove your bag
Yes...yes...yes
Then what do you do?
What do I do?
Fuck! I say
Will you stop it?
I'm not two, you know
I'm a fucking grown man!
Silence

What do you do? She says
I get my soft wipes...I say
And then? She says
And then, I say...
Oh God! Oh bollocks!
I'm falling...I'm falling
And then? She says
And then...I say
Oh God!
I wet them
What? Says she
I wet them, I say
Quietly, head bowed
You wet them, she says
I...wet...them
Yes, I wet them
I'm down
I'm done
I'm on the deck
My race is run
Your honour, she says
I'm sunk without trace
Your honour, she says
I rest my case

My Penis

Nerve damage, he said
Tugging rather aggressively
At my miserable member
Trying to return some life
To this shy and retiring creature
Stretches
Pull ups
Nothing
He was not responding
I was lying on the consultant's couch
Pants round my ankles
Again
He stopped tugging
Rinsed his hands
Mmm yes, he said, two options
One – his thumb tapped the keypad
Revealing
In close up profile
An enormous resting penis
About a mile long
With considerable bollocks
At its base
A hand appeared
Grabbed the bollocks
Squeezing
Several times
Quite magically
The penis perked up
And up!
To a remarkable height
The shot widening a little
To take in
This magnificent sight
My watering eyeballs
Did much the same thing

Was half expecting
A giant vagina
To wander in
Grinning
Is this the dawn
Of prescription porn, I wondered
Give it a go
So...we fit a pump, he said
In your scrotal sac
Oh! Do you...okay, I said
(I didn't know what to say, really)
Then...suddenly
I saw the future
Battling world domination
Of penile penetration
A job for Super Nob!
Back on screen
Another squeeze
And the giant penis
Stood at ease
Alternatively, he said
Producing a loaded syringe
Beaming
We can inject
Into the shaft
Shit! The shaft? I said
He tugged once more
And tapped the 'shaft'
At the aft (as it were)
Shall we give it a go?
Erm...I suppose so, I said
In for a penny
In went the needle, Aaagh!
The erection injection!
Should do the trick, he said

Was willing him to say
Just a small prick
But sadly
He didn't
So, now we wait
Back in ten, he said
Closed the curtain
And fled
I laid there
Gazing down at the wizened one
Once the proud collaborator
In the making
Of three golden girls
Now look at you, I said
A shadow of yer former!
Five minutes passed
Nothing
Not a peep
Not a squirm
Think he'd fallen asleep
Shook him about a bit
Go on my son, I said
One for the team!
But he wasn't having it
Yer little fucker, I said
I was getting a bit annoyed, to be honest
Everything I've done for you, I said
And what do you do?
The first chance you get
You throw in the towel
Call yourself a penis? I said
Yer pathetic
The doc returned
Just in the nick
Was about to get violent

He pulled back the curtain
Ah yes, oh dear, he said
Prodding
Tugging
Comatose, I said
A little morose
Yes, so I see, he said
Never guaranteed
That leaves you with the implant, I'm afraid
If you want to get laid
He chuckled
Have a think, he said
I needed a drink
Headed for the boozer
Head in a spin
Then...
Crossing Wigmore Street...
Something stirring
In my groin
Oh no! Not now! I groaned
Not in the fucking street
Please...sorry, I said
I take it all back mate!
Yer the best fucking penis ever!
Don't do this to me!
Walking became a difficulty
Could see him stood there
Proud
In my underwear
Smirking
The sick fucker
Stumbled into the pub
Found the loo
What to do?
Tried bashing it with my Bic

Made it worse!
Decided to douse it
In cold water
But what if someone walks in?
What will they think?
Seeing me wrestling with my erection
Trying to get the bastard
Into the sink!
An arrestable offence, probably
Drunk in charge of a drugged up penis
I saw the needle marks, your honour
I'd be a gonna
Thankfully...the water torture worked
The bugger
Gradually
Spluttering
Subsided
Sat in the bar
Large glass of Rioja(h)
Bag of nuts
Ah! Lovely
Had that think
Had that drink
Had another think
Had another drink!
Didn't fancy the nuts
Fuck, I thought
It's come to this
To pump or not to pump
To hump or not to hump
What to do eh?
What to do
But...
You know what
That's personal, that is

Well...
You have to draw the line somewhere
After all!
So...
I'm gonna keep it to myself
Whatever it is I do
If you don't mind
If that's okay
And I'm not going to share it
With you!
Nothing personal

Another Beautiful Summer's Day

I wake
Four thirty
Darkness
Stillness
Aching
Still night
That silence
Before the birds
Not feeling right
Baking hot
Shaking
With the cold!
My bag
On my belly
My bag!
On my belly!
Bulging
Ballooning! (A mini Zeppelin)
Fuck! Oh no! Oh God!
It's gonna blow!
Make for the loo...
Stubbing my toe
On the bed as I go
Aaaaargh! Shit!
Bag changing kit in hand...
Nervous
Steady...steady!
Lay out the bits
New stoma bag...ready
Soft wipes...ready
Water bowl...ready
Waste bag...ready
Removal spray
In hand...ready
I squirt

Lift the bag
From my belly
Steady...steady
Next thing I know...
I'm in an explosive overflow
Situation
Fuuuuuuck!!

Liquid shit flying everywhere
The walls, the ceiling, the bath, the door
The sink, the bathroom cabinet
The mirror, the radiator
The toilet
Not in it (sadly)
On it!
The glass shower screen
The slatted wooden bathmat
The pedal bin, the scales, the towel rack, the towels
The toilet roll...the toilet roll?
The cotton wool balls, the bleach, the flannel
The Bluebell Water Lily handwash
The Max White Colgate toothpaste
My toothbrush...euraaagh!
The Unicorn Candy bath foam
The Fenjal shower mousse
The Essential Waitrose limescale remover
The Febreze air freshener
Out of reach...unfortunately
The Argan Moroccan Rose soap
The Coconut Milk shampoo
The Brazilian LOVE bath and shower gel
The Mega Aussie conditioner
The Teatree and Cedarwood beard shampoo
For grizzly beards!
The Comforting Sanctuary Spa

White Lily and Damask Rose shower burst
The pumice stone
The new stoma bag
The soft wipes
The water bowl
The removal spray
The waste bag
Not in it (sadly)
On it!
The bag changing kit-bag
The Father Christmas rubber fucking duck
And ME!!
Everywhere!
I stand there
Frozen
I don't know what to do
I don't know what to do!
(Don't have a fucking clue)
I just stand there
Pyjamas round my ankles
Like manacles
Shivering a bit (obviously)
Marooned
In a sea of my own shit
Alone
Silent

Somewhere
In the distance
A songbird sings
As another
Beautiful
Summer's day
Begins

THE FUCKING SCARY VIRUS DIARIES
THE BEGINNING...

The Problem

Popped into our mini Sainsbury's
This morning
To get a paper
A bottle of Rioja
And a pint of milk
Essentials
There was a young lady
At the coffee machine
Blocking my passage (as it were)
Couldn't get past
Without
Possibly
Brushing
Her arse
Not safe (in every respect!)
Excuse me, I said
Politeness oozing from every pore
Could you move please
So I can get past
No, she said
I'm getting a coffee
Please, I said
In disbelief
No, she said
Can't you see
I'm getting a coffee!
There's plenty of room
It's meant to be
Two metres, I said
Come on, we all have to
Play the game
She huffed
And flattened herself against the coffee machine
Giving a clearance
Arsehole to gondola

Of maybe one foot six
To two foot
I left
No paper
No Rioja
No pint of milk
No essentials
And...
Fucking upset
Actually

24TH MARCH 2020:
Oh My God!...Fucking Hell!

Oh my God!
Fucking hell!
Prince Charles
Has got a very mild version
Of that virus
Named after a kiddies' fizzy drink
He is holed up in a castle somewhere
A nightmare
And soo lonely
When yer not very ill
Some arse
From the Daily Mail
Came on the Today programme
And told the delightful Martha Carney
That the Prince
Gave up
Shaking hands
Weeks ago
He shakes hands
For a living apparently
Charles's mother
Mrs Phillip

Who is one hundred and sixty one
(A 3 dart finish:
Treble top, treble 17, bull)
And should probably
Be dead anyway
Does not have
A mild version
Of the fizzy kiddy virus
As Donald Trump might say
She and her husband
Mr Phillip
Are holed up
In a different castle somewhere
A nightmare
And soooo lonely
When yer not even ill
We have been getting
This deeply upsetting headline news
About every fifteen minutes
Since half five this morning
I have just heard it again
On the news at noon
They still have
A mild version of the virus
Or no virus at all
And they are still holed up
In their various castles
And they are still
Soooo lonely
In their nightmares
I imagine
If I had a shotgun
And an arse
I would probably
Shove that shotgun
Up that arse
And end it all

I Think

I think
The birds
On my patio
Mr and Mrs Blackbird
Robin Redbreast
An extremely fat pigeon
And two tits
Are self isolating
The bird feeder
Hanging from
My ornamental flowering cherry
On the patio
Has not been
Nibbled at for over a week
Talking of tits
The small crowd
Of trainee doctors
Standing elbow to elbow
Laughing and joking
Outside Great Ormond Street Hospital
On Wednesday morning
Could learn a thing or two
From them
Birds
I think

28TH MARCH 2020:
I Have to Say

Our Prime Minister
Boris Johnson
Has got Coronavirus
I have to say
When I heard
I was
Really pleased
Appalling I know
However
I feel better
Now
I've come clean
But
I have to say
I still
Feel
The same way

2ND APRIL 2020:
The End of the Fucking World

Out on the street
This morning
I began to wonder
If me
And the six people
And the baby in a pram
And the fat ugly dog
I passed
In Bloomsbury Square
From a distance
Of at least two metres, obviously

And the number 38 bus driver
In his empty bus
And the Domino Pizza cyclist
And the Royal Mail van man
And the Tesco van man
And the Everyday waste disposal men
And the red Datsun car driver
And the frightened old lady
In the second floor window
I saw
On my way to Sainsbury's
To buy
Essentials
Paper, Rioja, milk
And a beer
Were
The last people
And the last fat ugly dog
And the last baby in a pram
Alive
On earth
So I sat on a bench
Wondered further
If all fifteen of us
Should gather
Now
Here
In Bloomsbury Square
Two metres apart obviously
Can't afford to lose anyone else
At this stage
And make a plan
For the future of mankind
But when I looked up
To gather my flock
Fuck!
I was totally alone
Not one person
Not one fat ugly dog

Not one baby in a pram
Even the frightened old lady in the window
Had disappeared
It was
Just me
On my own
Very much alone
No point going to Sainsbury's now, I mumbled
Went home
My wife was still there!
Alive
Making sardines on toast
My grandson was still in bed
Asleep
The remains of his 2am feast
Macaroni cheese and frankfurters
Congealed by his side
And Coco the cat
Who was also asleep
In my place
On the sofa
Just the four of us
Left
In the world
Not exactly Adam and Eve
But it's a start

A Dilemma

The one-legged man
Waiting for the green man
At the crossing
Was having a lot of trouble
With the two metre rule
Very wobbly
Very tall
Very pissed
The lights changed
The one-legged man
Lost his footing
That being his only foot
And fell
Heavily
The lady
Approximately two metres away
In the orange beret
Ordinarily
In that distant
Non virusy world
May well have rushed to help
She lurched forward
Then lurched back
Then froze
Hands stretched out
In a catching pose
I was able
To look on
From a superior critical standpoint
As poet in residence
With hernia issues
And do
Nothing
And walk away

Pen poised
I'm not sure
I have to say
I come out of this poem
Terribly well!

I Have to Say 2

Fuck!
Our Prime Minister
Boris Johnson
Has been taken into
Intensive Care
That's serious
I mean, he could die
I didn't want him dead
I just liked the idea
It has to be said
Of him suffering a bit
Like the masses of people
Suffering
And dying
On a daily basis
Under
His leadership

The Beauty

At 4.52am approximately
This morning
My very beautiful daughter
Seonaid
(One of three
Very beautiful daughters)
With the help
Of beautiful midwife Jonny
Her beautiful man
Gave birth
In their bedroom
Somewhat more swiftly
Than she had in mind
To a beautiful baby girl
By name of
Dolores Joy
While
Slightly emotional beautiful Grandma Gina
And slightly more emotional
Beautiful daughter Constance
Nervously listened in
(At least two metres away, obviously)
From across the hall
Beautiful baby Dolores
Cried
Eager for an early brekker
Beautiful euphoric Seonaid
Equally eagerly
Sorted brekker
One she had to hand
That she'd prepared earlier
Beautiful midwife Jonny
Who
Up until approximately 4.30am

Had just been plain beautiful Jonny
With beautiful daughter Constance
And beautiful Grandma Gina
(Two metres away, obviously)
Looked on
In awe and wonder
And a few joyous tears
As the paramedics
Arrived
Having just missed
This extraordinary moment
Of
The beauty

My Neighbour

On returning
From an essential Sainsbury's shop
Paper, wine, milk
And a beer
Bumped into my neighbour
Dan
A man
Who enjoys a drink
I say bumped
More
We saw
Each other from
Several metres away
And closed down
To
Two metres, approximately
Obviously
He in the middle of the road
Me safely on the kerb

On the north side
Of Bloomsbury Square
We chatted
The usual stuff
Corona
Boris
Loathe that fuckin' fuck
To quote my neighbour
Matt fucking Hancock
To quote me
An empty number 14 bus
Squeezed between us
I waved to the driver
He waved back
With a smile
Wonders wonders
After
A manoeuvre
Around a crimson headed jogger
Determined to breathe on me
The conversation got
Serious
So...
(The word of the moment)
What time are you opening the bar
Ce soir? I asked
Five Bob, he said
Without hesitation
I hang on till six, I said
Can't do it Bob, he said
I'm two Estrella Galicias in by then
With a couple more
Lined up
Thus opening the door
For that goblet of Rioja
With supper
Ah!...but Bob, he said
Suddenly intense
Intimate

Conspiratorial
The two metre rule under threat
What I do like, he said
Is Spanish brandy
It just makes me feel
So much better, he said
The very thought
Visibly
Filling him with joy
We laughed
I'll drink to that, I said

I Have to Say 3

Our Prime Minister
Boris Johnson
Is out of Intensive Care!
Along with
The Queen
Stanley, his dad
Dominic Raab
Matt Hancock
Ten year old
Rishi Sunak
Donald Trump
Nicky fucking Campbell
The Daily Mail
And endless
Obsequious
Commentators and journalists
I have to say
Our prayers have been answered
That's such a huge relief

Community Spirit

Was watering my window boxes
From the open window
Not that surprisingly
No cars
No buses
No bikes
No one
Eerie – The Movie
Just an early spring bumble bee
Buzzing
Around my mini fruit trees
On the steps
That have never produced
Any fruit
Ever
Then a man
With a bag
And a mask
And a fag
Dangerous!
Appeared
Life!
Almost overwhelmed with excitement
I raised my hand
Gave a wave
Morning! I called
Grinning hugely
He stopped
Looked round at me
Hi! I called again
Wave retreating
Grin subsiding
He looked behind himself
At the museum railings
Then back at me

Quizzically
Do I know you? He growled
No, I called, just being friendly
In these troubled times
Oh! He said
And did a funny thing with his head
A sort of shake and a nod
All in one
Then he turned
Gently collided with a small tree
And continued on
At a pace

12TH APRIL 2020:
I Have to Say 4

Our Prime Minister
Boris Johnson
Is out of hospital
On Easter Sunday
The son of Stanley
He is risen
From the almost dead!
Let's hope
He wanders about a bit
As is traditional
But not for too long
Then
Ascends
I have to say
To somewhere
A fuck of a long way
From here

Queue

Was in the queue
Two metres apart, obviously
For the butcher's
One in, one out
The lady in front of me
On the phone
Telling a tearful tale of death
Five weeks in
And nothing had changed
Two blokes
Possibly pissed
Brushed past me
One of them
Swaggered to
Second place in the queue
He looked round
Beaming
Willing a response
I glared
He wilfully coughed
His ruddy faced mate
Giggled
I glared
Come on! He shouted
Grinning
Open mouthed
Reluctantly
I looked away
Along with everyone else
The two goons
Disappeared into the chippy
Next door
Laughing hysterically
We continued to queue
As if nothing had happened

I Have to Say 5

Our Prime Minister
Boris Johnson
Has had a baby
Well...
His girlfriend
Whose name escapes me
Has
Another distraction
They've named him Wilfred
After the actor
Who played the rag and bone man
Albert Steptoe
In the legendary 60's sitcom

P.S.
It's just come to me
Boris's girlfriend
Is called Carrie
Named after the character
Brilliantly played by Cissy Spacek
In the deeply disturbing
Blood soaked
Legendary 70's horror film
Of the same name

Passed By

Morning, I said
Breezily
As I stepped into the road
For the two metre avoid
Of the oncoming person
Morning? He said
Yes, hello, I said
Morning!
Why are you talking to me? He said
No one ever talks to me
I talk to everyone, I said
Andy...Andy Grafton, he said
Hello Andy, I said
I'm Bob
You said hello to me! He said
I'm not a tramp
I'm nearly a tramp, he said
But I lost someone
And then...I...
Lost it...a bit
Why did yer talk to me!? He said
Almost getting angry
It's the same here, yer see
All the time
Up in Manchester it's...
It's friendlier, I said
Yeah he said, yeah yeah fucking...
Sorry, he said
Getting quite physical
They fucking talk to me!
Are you a lecturer? He said
No, I said, I'm an actor
An actor? He said, oh oh oh!
He grinned all toothless
I've worked in Manchester, I said

It's a very friendly city
Was it a film? He said
No, a play, I said
But was it on film? He said
No, it was on stage
It was just on, I said
I froze in a pose
Then it was gone!
I unfroze from my pose
Ah! He said
But it's in your head eh?
He smiled
All gums
Yes, I said, it's in my head
I was suddenly moved
I tossed him a pound coin
Sorry, I said, lying
That's all I've got
He snatched it
Out of the air
Like the Sobers-esque slip fielder
He probably once was
In his native Jamaica
See you Andy, I said
Look after yourself
Thanks Bob, he said
You spoke to me man!
Take care, I said
He stumbled up the street
I watched him
In despair
Thinking
Fuck!
Should have given him that tenner
I felt it nestled in my pocket
When I found
The pound
What a fucking world eh?

We're Fucked!

We're fucked!
We're fucked!
We're all fucked!
I'm fucked!
You're fucked!
The fucking government's fucked!
We're all fucked!
Yelled the angry young man
Into his mobile phone
In Bloomsbury Square
Looking around
Breathing heavily
Eyes blazing
Ready to take on allcomers
I ducked behind a statue
Of Charles James Fox
(The Magna Carta in hand)
Just in case
He thought I was fucked
As well
Can you hear me man? He screamed
This appeared to produce
A reply
He was, quite obviously
Not happy with
Fucking what!!
Man, you're fucked too man! He screamed
Yer not with me
Can't you see
We're all fucked!
I peeped out from behind the statue
As his expressive back was passing
The All Star Bowling Alley
Then stopping
At the crossing

From where I just caught
His final thought
If that's what you think man, he screamed
You can fuck off!!

Next Time

That's a great look
Said the man on crutches
Two metres away approximately
Waiting at the lights
On the Gray's Inn Road
Thanks, I said
Yer like a cross between
Willy Nelson and...
Someone else, he said
Thanks, I said
I'd love to take a photo of you, he said
I take photos
Can I take a photograph of you?
Yes, I said
Have you got a camera? I asked
No, he said
Then we have a problem, I said
Yeah, he said
Chuckling
Wobbling
Next time, I said
Yeah, he said, next time
Would be good
Don't forget your camera, I said
As he stumbled off
Good idea, he chuckled
That's a great look
I watched him go

Thinking
Sadly
There probably won't be
A next time

Desperate

I'm sorry, I'm sorry, she pleaded
I'm a mess, I know
You're fine, I said
To the young woman
On the street
Outside my flat
Please don't go away, she said
I'm not, I'm here, I said
Don't worry
I'm only wearing these, she said
Pointing at
Her fluffy dirty pink carpet slippers
'Cos I fell asleep
In the street
And someone stole my shoes
Fuck, I said
Yeah I know, she said
I gave her a tenner
Her face lit up
Thank you, she said
Hope it helps, I said
I can get two nights
In the hostel with this
She ran off
Alive and happy
Made my
Isolated day

The Lady in Russell Square

Morning, I said
To the lady with the very red lips
And the shopping trolley
In Russell Square
Oh morning, she said
You're Megan's dad aren't you?
No, I'm not, I said
Oh, she said
I'm Gemma's dad
And Seonaid's dad
And Sophie's dad
I said
Oh sorry, she said
I used to work in a school
And I thought
You were Megan's dad
Oh, no, sorry
Morgan's dad
Not Megan, Morgan, she said
No, I'm not his dad either, I said
Smiling
She looked baffled
Anyway...
Nice to meet you, I said
Oh and you, she said
And on we went

5TH JUNE 2020:
Woodstock

Woodstock's that way man
Said the man
Pointing westward
In the porkpie hat
Flower shirt
And fading stripey jacket
Pardon? I said
Woodstock's that way, he said
With a matey gurgle
Thanks man, I said
I'll see you there

10TH JUNE 2020:
Anniversary

A year ago
Today
I had my arse
Removed
Surgically
And
A substantial
Portion
Of my large
Bowel
Was also
Amputated
Now my arse
Pokes out
Of my tummy
Funny
(If it weren't so personal)

Where a bag
Awaits
The 'output'

If it happened today
The surgeon would have to
Operate
From two metres away
And
Who knows
Where my arse
Would have ended up

16TH JUNE 2020:
Hearse

A hearse
Drove past me
On Guilford Street
The undertaker
Looked my way
Waved
Seemed to smirk
Then pointed ahead
Nodding
As if to say
I'll see you there
Does he know
Something
I don't know?

First Pint

Please wait to be seated
Said the notice
By the door
Of The Plough
I waited
Please hand san
Another notice
I hand sanned
Splashing cleansing gloop
On my groin
In the process
What would you like sir?
The masked barman called out
Probably smiling
From behind the Perspex sheeting
I followed the one way arrows
To the bar
Furiously
Rubbing away
With my paper mask
At the unfortunate wet patch
By my zip
Ah! Hello, I said
Hello sir, he said
You all right there?
Yes, well...no, I said
Scanning the pumps
I'd like a pint of Abbot please, I said
A request
I had been imagining since late March
I would never utter again
The Abbot's off sir, I'm afraid sir, he said
Ah! Right, shit! Sorry...well
Scanning again
A pint of Tribute then, I said
The Tribute is off I'm afraid sir, as well sir, he said

Is it? I said, bristling slightly
Do you have any ales? I asked
Mild tension
Colouring my natural bonhomie
Oh yes sir, the IPA sir, he said
The IPA?
Why didn't you say
The IPA
Was the only beer you had on today?
I didn't know what you wanted sir, he said
A deep breath
He pulled my beer
Are you new here? I asked
No sir, he said
This is my local, I said
I don't remember seeing you
I've been here since late March sir, he said
But the pub's been closed since then, I said
I know sir, he said
Sensing the conversation
Was going nowhere
I paid
And made my way
Along the arrows
To the 'Exit' door
And sat
At a small table
Awaiting delivery of my beer
Miles from another table
On a desolate windy street
Thinking
I've been looking forward to this moment
For one hundred and eight days
Fuck!

The Steps

Stood at the top
Directly below me
Stood the masked man
20 steps
Separated us
From full on
Covid collision
We clocked each other
Decision time
He stepped to his left
And stepped up a step
As I stepped to my right
And stepped down a step
Without exchanging glances
We both knew
The chances
Of that fateful meeting
Were increasing
He swiftly stepped
To his right
And stepped up another step
As I, not so swiftly
Stepped to my left
And stepped another step down
Shit!
There were now
Only 16 steps
Separating us
From total carnage
He pointed left
I pointed left
And gazelle like
He stepped a nimble two-step
Diagonally up
As I

More clown-like
Stepped a stumbly two-step
Diagonally down
Disaster averted
He leapt on up
As I clowned on down
As we passed, I said
I thought we were on
For a full on head on
I know, said the masked man
In a broad Scottish brogue
Well, it's Saturday!
He turned to me
And grinned
I think

The Blind Man, the Tan and the Can

The blind man
Stood at the counter
Buying his shopping
2 metres behind him, approximately
Stood the heavily tanned lady
Chatting
On her shocking pink mobile phone
2 metres behind her, approximately
Stood me
Laden with fresh bread, Earl Grey tea
The ripest tomatoes, Basil
And the essential
Chilled Chilean Naciente
Suddenly, the Tan exclaimed
Could be some time
I'm behind a man
Pretending to be blind
With a white stick
I audibly gasped
The Tan swung round
Mimicked my gasp
Rolled her wild eyes
And left

Walking back through St Andrew's Gardens
Heading towards
The Gray's Inn Road
2 red faced men
Were sat on a bench
Cans in hand
The more pissed man said
Excuse me, have you got any change?
Need 46p for my next can
No sorry, 44p

Gave him a quid
I admired his honesty
That's for your next can, I said
And 56p for your next can
After the next can
Thanks Colonel, he said
I'm in for a long day!
I'll say, I said, enjoy
Oh I most certainly will, he said
Casually tossing his empty can over his head
Into the bin
Good shot! I said
I'm well practiced Colonel, he cackled
As I moved on
Towards the Gray's Inn Road

Speechless

Collecting fungi? I enquired
Of the nose ringed man
Fiddling
With the bark of a big tree
In Russell Square
What? He replied
I repeated
No, no, no, he said
It's bits of pineapple
For the squirrels
Vits
Give 'em a drink
And a few nuts
Left me speechless
He placed another pineapple chunk
In a crevice
As I stumbled over a passing dog
And beat a hasty

20TH SEPTEMBER 2020:
Miserable Men

Said good morning
To the miserable man
On a bench
In Bloomsbury Square
He looked up
Stared at me
His lips didn't move
I moved on
An ugly fat dog
Was having a shit

On the grass
As I passed
His miserable owner
Looked on
Good morning, I said
Eeerrgh, he said
I moved on
By the gate
I passed a pigeon
Standing proud on a bread roll
Morning, I said
Good morning, he chirped
Enjoy yer breakfast, I said
Oh yes, it's my favourite, he chirped
Taking a large beakful
As I turned left
On to Bloomsbury Way

It's Not Easy

Sitting in the basement
Of University College Hospital
Awaiting my first blast
Of radiotherapy
Hoping they can zap
Some nasty little lymph nodes
That have taken root
On my right pelvic wall
Very thin man opposite
Not looking very well
Keen to chat
We're all going to die
He tells me, with a smile
Not for a while, I hope, I reply
With a grimace
From behind my mask
An over happy nurse appears
Wanting me to drink
Gallons of water
Swelling of the bladder
Helps to expose
The nasty little nodes, she tells me
Beaming
I hurl it down my neck
And wait
Brave masked faces
Surround me
In the troubling gloom
Of bright fluorescent light
A very ill man
Passes by in a bed
All drips and drains
Turning
Glaring at me
Pain and terror
Fill his misty eyes

I wait
And wait
Finding it almost impossible
Not to think
Dark thoughts
Fucking hell
It's not easy

The Two Road Sweeps

Two road sweeps
In Red Lion square
Then you fucking come
And fucking pick
Them fucking up! Said one
Sorry, said the other
You shithead! Said one
Just trying to 'elp mate,
Said the other
But they were *my* fucking
Leaves! Yelled one
I'm sorry! Said the other
Shithead! Yelled one
Kicking his cart
In frustration

Again

Thought
It had stopped
So I put down me Bic
And then...
It started
Again
More people getting sick
Again
More people getting
Dead
Again
Then...
All locked in
Again
I might just have to
Go back to bed
And stay there
Until I get dead
In a non virusy
Way
Naturally
You might say

It's the Weekend!

Not a sound on the street
This morning
Just a solitary giant dried up leaf
Tumbling across the road
And the obligatory empty number 14 bus
It's the seventeenth day
Of lock down 2
Not easy
Met Alex the Scot
In Bloomsbury Square
He was waiting to
Collect some curtains at three
It was only half nine!
He'd just had a McDonalds McMuffin thing
With a couple of hash browns
On the side –
Normally have one
Today I had two
A wee treat, he said
Left the square
Crossed the road
At the green man
Misjudged the kerb
And went sprawling
Aaarrgh! I cried
Ripped my jeans
Cut my hand and knee
A passing saint
Collected my hat
As I struggled to my feet
Are you okay? She asked
With a worried smile
Passing me my hat
From approximately 2 metres, obviously
Aaarrgh! I said

Sorry, yes, thank you
She smiled some more worry
And, hesitantly, went on her way
I limped to a bench
In Red Lion Square
In a certain amount of pain
And wrote this poem
Smudging oozing blood
On my Pukka pad
In the process
Not a great start
To the weekend

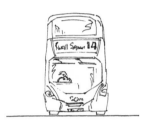

8TH DECEMBER 2020:
The Greatest

We have a vaccine!
We have a vaccine!
And we
The self proclaimed
Greatest nation in the world
With the greatest
Jabologists
In the world
Have come up with it...

First!
Of course!
Ahead of all the other
Somewhat inferior stupid nations
Mrs Old from Coventry
Who is one hundred and sixty-one
(A Three dart finish:
Treble top, treble 17, bull)
Was the first person
In the world
To get the jab
At 6.31 this morning
Approximately
Injected
In her upper left arm
We were told
By one of our greatest nurses
In the world
While more flashing cameras
Than you've 'ad 'ot dinners
Flashed
We watched
Mesmerised
As Mrs Old was wheeled through
A cheery clappy
Greatest nurses in the world guard of honour
With Mrs Old
Quite obviously wondering
What the fuck
Was going on

The Treeman

Hanging
Out of the window
Cutting and pruning
The fading and shivering
Hydrangeas, geraniums, fuschias
And chillies
In the window box
A 'Pines and Needles'
Christmas tree man
In his dirty white van
And matching overalls
Was delivering a beauty of a tree
Next door
He gave me a nod
As I busied
I nodded a smile back
Next thing I knew
He flew up my steps
Beaming
Thrusting a mini beauty
In my face
Across the railings
I think you may need one of these, he said
Oh, thanks mate, I said
A tad taken aback
He turned away
Then...swung back round
Suddenly angry
Aggressively
Jabbing a pointy finger at me
And don't you forget, he snarled
To come down my chimney
On Christmas eve!
I will be there mate, I said, relieved
He raised an eyebrow

Unconvinced
And with a jovial festive wave
He sped off towards Russell Square
As I set my weeny tree
In the decimated icy compost

Tiers before Deadtime

Tier 24
Means
No one can go
Out the door
Anymore
Ever
So...
To coin a word
When
The food
And the booze
And the loo roll
And the Christmas cake
Run out
The game's up
But
At least
We won't
Die
Of
The Virus

Biopsy

Masked up
Dressed up
In a chilly hospital corridor
Awaiting
A prostate biopsy
Saw a witty anaesthetist
Unaware
There
Was no arsehole
About my person
I'd had it removed
A while ago now
That being the very arsehole
Up which
The normal procedure
Would normally proceed
Seems
A specialist
Radiologist
Was required
In order to locate
My prostate
With a large needle
Via the scrotal area
Ouch!
She, I'm afraid to say
Is busy, said the anaesthetist
Wittily
And cannot be with us before lunch
It was now breakfast time
Or small beaker of water time
In my case
A cool American urologist
Called by
Asking me

Hey, if I was me
I said I was
He apologised
Asking
Hey, what was I reading
To pass the time
A memoir, I said
By Gabriel Byrne
The Irish film star
He'd never heard of Gabriel Byrne
The Irish film star
Four hours later
Shivering
I clambered up
On the operating table
Mysterious gowned figures
All around
Busying
With stuff
Chattering
About stuff
(Didn't seem to notice me!)
Leg stirrups being attached
A smiley lady
In search
Of a vein
As a gas mask
Covered my mouth...

Am now
Home in bed
In cosy pain
Munchin' on the paracetamol
And a corned beef and chutney sarny
Passing, sadly
On the large glass of Rioja
I could happily inhale
Awaiting
The results

Of the biopsy
In twelve plus one
Days time

10TH JANUARY 2021:
The Dream

Woke up
Shaken, terrified
Bathed in sweat
I'd been back
Somewhere
Mel Smith
Was there
An old star
Masses of white hair
(He was nearly bald
When last alive)
Standing there
Dressed for winter
With an ornate cane
All Orson Welles-ish
In the blazing sunshine
On a hillside
By an isolated theatre
People milling around
Star gazers
In awe
I'm in our play
I've done before
Coming back
After many years
With great expectations
Fuck! I'm on!
Making it all up
As I go along

Very frightening
I know I'm making it up
And it's shit
And I'm getting away
With it!
Mel
Looking on
Like God
Now, suddenly
I'm in the audience
In this vast arena
In this blackness
Waiting for the lights
To come up
At the end of our play
About to see
Me
Dying
But the lights
Don't come up
It's getting darker
And darker
The show is over
Why is it getting darker?
I ask, in a whisper
In the silence
No applause
No one here
I'm alone
Frozen in fear...
Now...
A twinkling...
Sparkling, shimmering...
Like...
Like millions
Of distant fairy lights
Getting brighter
The play is over
I'm not there

Such a relief
It's all going to be okay, I say
Back to normal
I wake up
I think
Strange feeling
In my head
Think I may well
Have gone bonkers
Am I awake? I whisper
I can see the clock
Twenty past five
I must be awake
I've never been so pleased
To see a clock
In all my life!
Sit up in bed
Bathed in sweat, as I say
Stinging my eyes
Gina is there
Gina is there!
Next to me
Awful dream, I say
Very scary
Mel was there
Would I like a cup of tea? She asks me
I'll be fine, I say
Head to the loo
To change my very full bag
I've been shitting myself
Now, I'm wondering
As I drink my tea
If I'll be normal again
I'm coming back, I say
Good, says Gina
Drink your tea
Can I have another biscuit? I ask
(That's normal, I think)
Of course, says Gina

Thanks my darling, I say
She holds my hand
I feel better now

Hundreds and Thousands

Started doing
News reports
From mortuaries
Now!
Pictures
Stainless steel racks
All
Ready
Awaiting
The hundreds and thousands –
Not sparkly decoration
On top
Of a cup cake
Or trifle –
Bodies
In bags
Thousands of them
Truly
Fucking
Horrific

A Moment

This lady
Was standing
In front of a tree
In Bloomsbury Square
She put down her knapsack
Her tote bag
And her Sainsbury's meal deal
Very delicately
Stepped forward
And gave it a great big hug
Turning her head
Her cheek nuzzling up to the bark
Like a lover
Nutter
Would have been my reaction
Pre virus
Pre lock down
Not now
Somehow
It made sense

Alex the Scot

Saw Alex the Scot again
This morning
On his bench in Bloomsbury Square
Strummin' on a ukulele
Hello Bob, it is Bob isn't it? he said, all perky
Didn't get those curtains, you know
She didn't show
Oh dear, I said, remembering back
To our last encounter
Nice uke', I said
Oh yes, he said, holding it aloft
Got it off this man
On the first of Jan
In the Kings Cross area
Wanted eighty, gave him seventy
Bargain eh? He said
And he burst into
A swift refrain
Of the Bing Crosby classic
Every time it rains, it rains
Pennies from heaven
Beautiful, I said, great voice
Oh, no no no can't sing can't sing, he said
How's yer cancer?
Not good, I said, it's come back
Sorry to hear that Bob, he said
But yer know what they say?
If yer get it, you've got it
Yer know what I'm sayin'?
And he burst into song
Every time it rains, it rains
Pennies from heaven
Saving me a reply
I just didn't have

Incurable

Multiple nodes, she said
Multiple nodes? I replied
Yes, I'm afraid so, she said
Consulting her screen
A lot of new ones, it seems
Right pelvis, left pelvis
Middle right back −
But the right middle back, I said
Were already there
There's new ones, she said
New ones, I said, as well as the old ones?
Yes, she said, a cluster
A cluster? I said
And there's also one
Not pausing for breath
In your lung
My lung? I said
A small one, yes, she said
In my lung!?
'Fraid so, she said
Shit, I said
Sorry, I said
Which means...she said
It's incurable
Incurable? I said
Yes, It's in your bloodstream now
My bloodstream
I was trying to take this in
By repeating back
Everything she said
Which seemed to be working
So, I said...
(That word again −
Probably acceptable under the circs)
Are you saying...this is going to get me?

Well...She said
She took a deep breath –
Is it terminal? I said
Trying to sound casual
As if enquiring about the weather
I don't like to say terminal
It's treatable
We can treat it, she said
But you can't cure it, I said
We can't cure it, she said
Shit, I said
Again
Sorry
Again
Stood
On Huntley Street
Ten minutes later
Removing my mask
Shivering
Wishing
The Marlborough Arms was open
(My old local
From RADA days)
So I could go
And sit
In a quiet bit
With my beer
(Or beers)
And a bag of nuts
Knowing my worst fears
Had just been realised
Then most probably get
Incredibly upset

MULTIPLE NODES

INCURABLE

BUT

TREATABLE

22ND JANUARY 2021:
Morning After

Just said
Good morning
To a new lamp post
In Bloomsbury Square
Just being friendly
Didn't reply
Miserable
Fucker

94

Sitting Here – It's Not Easy 2

Sitting here
Just sitting here
Waiting
Two and three quarter hours
So far
For a telephone appointment
With my urologist
Mr Grey
Who did say, recently
He prides himself
On punctuality
I had bowel cancer
Which was excised
Then returned
And was zapped
Then returned
All over the place
And now
I have prostate cancer
As well
Greedy bastard
You might say
So...
(I know!)
I'm waiting
(Three and a quarter hours now)
To talk to Mr Grey
About the way forward
Prostate wise
And I'm getting well pissed off
And writing about it
Is not exactly having the calming affect
I had in mind
Which is getting me
Even more
Pissed off, actually
Fucking hell...
It's not easy

Another Square

I'm in a square
Gordon square
A different square
To my normal squares
Crocuses peeping
Around the plane tree
Over there
Purple and yellow
Spring in the air
Just had
My Covid jab
My Covid swab
A giant cotton bud
Up my hooter
In my gob
Made me gag
Not nice
A glorious smile
From a passing young beauty
So open
So warm
Hi, she says
Hello, I say
And she's gone
Starting Chemo
On Friday
Two days away
Not that I'm counting
Not that I'm nervous
A milky sun is setting
Clouds are moving in
A little more weather
A little more winter
Is about to feature
Before the grey

Before the darkness
Moves away
But not
I suspect
Forever

✣ THE CHEMO TIMES ✣

5TH FEBRUARY 2021:
Friday

A vast room
Bright, sunny, airy
Welcoming, not scary
Large enough for cricket
(With a short boundary!)
Big comfy armchairs
Everywhere
Two metres apart, obviously
Occupied by people
All ages
All sizes
All sexes probably
(Seems to be
A lot to choose from these days)
All sitting
Masked up
Quietly
Some reading
Some staring vacantly
Some just...
Sitting
Mostly on drips

Cheery blue nurses
Scuttle
Lovingly, patiently
Tending their needy patients
I'm sitting
Quietly
Masked up
Bit sweaty
Reading
Nervously
Robert! Robert Goody!
Aaarrgh!
The call! That's me!!
Stick up my hand
Back at school
Sorry, I say, that's me! I'm here!!
I'm Gemma, says she
Oohhh!
A tot of human brandy
I'm here, says she
To take you thro'
Your chemotherapy
Thank you, I say, thank you
I'm Bob, I say
Hello Bob, says she
And she takes my arm
And I feel
Quite safe

Friday – Thoughts

Friday
Five twenty
In the morning
Dark and cold
Head in aspic
Pickled
Sitting
Again
On the sofa
In a position
Where I'm almost
Ache free
Mug of Earl Grey tea
Homemade choccy bic
Deeeelish
Tennis on the telly
Can't read my book
For some reason
Just wont go in
Diego Schwartzman
Getting hammered
By a qualifier
Flip over
To some comedy
I recorded
Not funny
Back to Diego
He's disappeared!
A loser I fancy
Out the window
A red sky at dawning
Much needed beauty
(Local shepherd, wont be happy)
I stand and stare
In wonder
Shivering

Snow still lingers
On the wilting avocado plants
In the compost heap
Back on the sofa
Always on the sofa
In position
Wrapped in a blanket
Like an old man
Which I suppose I am
Time for my pill
'Cos I'm ill
Seems to make me
Feel
Worse
And morose
Slice of toast
Glass of juice
There goes a number 14
Empty
As ever
Nick Kyrgios now playing
He's a tosser
Could be fun tho'
Could be
I'll have a bath
Some cosy bubbles
Put on
Some colourful clothes
Homemade rainbow socks
Huge, like fluffy paddles
May even brush my hair
Don't care anymore
Get this day
Underway
Can't wait
Nick has just won
The opening set
That's made me smile
The first in a while
Friday
Here I come

Saturday – Early Bird

Robins
Were tweeting
At half five this morning
Still dark
Early start
Like myself
Probably got
A busy day planned
Birdy fun
Make the most
Of the winter sun
Couple of worms
Tidy the nest
Quick fly
Stretch the wings
Off to the squares
Get some grubs in
Fer lunch
Then head off
For a long fly
In Regents Park
May even treat the chicks
To a pedalo
On the lake

Sunday – Valentine's Day

Having trouble
Coping
With the Chemo
Thickest of heads
Unable to think
Pain in the stoma
Gone off the drink
(A big worry)
Pins and needles
In my fingers and toes
Aching all over
Bleeding nose bleed
So tired, so tired
Heavy eyes
That refuse to cry
I wish they would
It might help!
Not that keen
To even sleep for long
Got a Valentine's card
From an 'Ardent admirer'
This morning
Cheered me up no end
Gina got one too
From an 'Admirer'
She also got designer chocs
In a red velvet heart shaped box
AND champagne
All I got was a bloody card
Bloody Chemo

Wednesday – My Head

4 am
My head!
My head!
Can't sleep
Out of bed
Upstairs
Open the curtains
Pretend it's morning
Open the windows
For the Covid chill
Take some pills
'Cos I'm ill
Kettle on
Cuppa tea
Choccy biccy
On the sofa
Safe
Plump the cushions
Fluffy paddles
Fer the pins and needles
Cosy, cosy
My head!
My head!
Fire on
Telly on
Tennis or foota?
Shit!
A huge decision
This early
Huge, impossible
Fuck!
Feed the cat
While I ponder
She looks astonished
Early solids!

She wont have to
Viciously
Attack my knee
To remind me later
Another cuppa tea
Back on the sofa
Relaxed
Them pills is workin'
Ready for tennis...
Or maybe...
Foota
My head!

On Tricia's Bench

Having
A five minute sit
On Tricia's bench
In Russell Square
A bench
Dedicated to our beautiful neighbour
Who left us
Three years ago
Too young to leave
We grieve...still
Having a moment
With her
Just had my second chemo
Plus steroids
(One to avoid, I feel)
Tired and wired
Eyes on stalks
Cross man with dog
Pissing on a log
(The dog
Not the man!)
And rolling in the mud
(The man
Not the dog!)
An oasis of crocuses
Gorgeous
(Yet to be pissed on!)
Clear blue sky
Runners stretching
Graceful Arabic chap
In a flat cap
Beaming, waving
Buds budding
Got left over Christmas hazel nuts
For the squirrels

In me pocket
Not a furry fucker
In sight
It's all lookin' lovely, Tricia, I say
Such a shame
You can't be here
To share it
With us
Today

Gemma's Non Birthday

It's Gemma's birthday
Today
Our beautiful eldest daught
She tells us
It's her non birthday
Still keen
However
To have lots of pressies
Serious tasty solids
And a magnificent
Homemade
Black forest Gateau
But we won't
Be putting
42 candles on it!
Not a word will be said
Happy Birthday
Our darling Gem

Fuck!

Fuck
5.20
Fuck
Just me
A cuppa tea
Some drugs
A biccy
Choccy
Obviously
And an empty
Number 14 bus
What more
Could a chap
Ask for?
Fuck!
There goes another one...

Fuck! 2

4.50
Ten to five
Shit!
Have to get up
My head is mental
Alive
Migraine
Without the pain
Unbearable
Something
Inside
Anguish
Torment
That's it!
Fuzzy...
Torment!
Not funny
No point in laying here
Tormented, fuzzy
Any longer
Have to get up
Heavy body
Knackered
Swing out the chilled feet
Blotchy, taught skin
Starting to tingle
Needles and pins
You okay darling? Says Gina
Stirring
All warm and gorgeous
In bed
Next to me
I'm fine, I say, I'm fine
It's just...my fucking head!
Go back to sleep, don't worry, I say

I'll be okay
Go up stairs
Cuppa tea
Choccy bic
Start the day
(Even tho' it's officially night)
Lovely
Turn off the light, I say
On with the dressing gown
The fluffy paddles
Gather
My book
My pills
'Cos I'm ill
Please don't worry Gina, I say
Again
I'll be okay
She's not convinced
See yer later
My darling...
I close the bedroom door...
Shit!
The non pain
Is gaining ground...
Now...
Up the stairs I go...
Them feet, them paddles
Firmly on the floor
Routine routine –
Kitchen, kettle, water, tea
I'll be okay, just me
Curtains, windows, lights
Start the day
I'm doin' okay!
Now...
Kitchen
Mug
Fridge
Milk

Mug
Teaspoon
Sugar
Mug
Teapot
Tea
Mug
Teaspoon
Stir
Done it!
A cup of tea!
Sorted!
Brilliant!
Easy
What's the problem here?
I'm okay
As I say
Feelin...
Terrific!
Soo much better
Sofa
Here I come...!
Fuck!
We're out of
Choccy bics
FUCK!!!

26TH FEBRUARY 2021:
Moon Ulcer

Just spied
The moon
Peepin'
Over the roofs
Opposite
Stunning

A wisp of cloud
Hovering
Protecting
The main man

Just spewed
Cetylpyridinium Chloride gel
On the oozin' sore
Creepin'
Over my lip
Protecting
Cooling
The throbbing

Of the two
The moon
Takes it
For me
Every time

27TH FEBRUARY 2021:
The Pits

It's ten
Past
4
And
I'm just
Not sure
How much
More
Of
This
Whatever
It is
I can

Take
To be honest
My
Poor old head
Is
Soo
Full
Of...
Something
Sooo full

I will
Go
And make
A
Cuppa
And
Then
I have to
Feel
Better
If
I don't
I really
don't
Know
What
To do
Fucking Chemo

Maybe
A choccy bic
Ah!
A good sign!

I think
This
Is
What

We
Call
A
Low point

Nearly an hour later...

It's Not Just Me, Is it?

Lady Gaga's
Beloved
Two French bulldogs
Koji and Gustav
Have been found
Apparently
Having been
Feared
Kidnapped
My heart is sick, she said
And she is hoping her family
Will be whole again
This was
The third
Most important
Item
Of news
On the news
At 5am
This morning

Following
A giant iceberg
The size
Of greater London
Apparently
That is
Adrift
All at sea
Somewhere

I just
Don't have
The words
But I think
It's not
Just me
That's
Going
Crazy
Thank fuck!

28TH FEBRUARY 2021:
Morning Stroll

Passed
Famous person
Gok Wan
Dark shades
Black tracksuit
Shocking pink head band
Cool
Jogging
In Bloomsbury Square
This fine morn
Slowly
Puffing, sweating
His mini bulldog
Dolly Albertine Dishcloth Wan
By name
Panting
Along behind

Ah! There you are! I said
For some reason
Good to see yer
And you, he said
Flashing a perfect set
Of gleaming white gnashers
He's put on weight, I whispered
When he'd passed
The dog? Said Gina
No! I said, Gok
That's why he's jogging, she said
Nice bloke, I said
He looked knackered

28TH FEBRUARY 2021:
Morning Stroll 2

This
Great big fat
Crow
In
Lincoln's Inn Fields
This fine morn
Was pecking
On a can
Of Red Bull
The big fat crow
Was obviously
Low
On energy

Spring

There's
A tiny tiny
Delicate green
Shoot
On my otherwise
Lean, leafless
Chilli plant
On our kitchen
Windowsill
That I have nursed
Thro'
This
Horrendous
Destructive
Winter
New life!
Has sprung
Fresh life
Has won thro'
It's a wonderful thing
Spring
I'm very 'appy

On Tricia's Bench 2

The superior hoity toits lady
With the coiffured
Blow dried
Poodle
Just about managed
To say
Good morning to me
This morning
It was such an effort
For her
To engage
With this hairy
Piece of low life
On Tricia's bench

Probably
Shouldn't have
Upset me
But it did!
And...
Two hours and twenty minutes later
It's still with me
As you can see!
Ridiculous

I'm Fed Up – Frustration

I'm
Fed up
It's ten past four
In the morning
And I'm up
Upstairs
On the sofa
In the lounge
In the dark
And it's...
Ten past fucking four!
In the fucking morning
And I should be asleep
But I can't be asleep
And I'm...up
On the bleedin' sofa
In the fucking lounge
In the fucking dark
'Cos it's the middle of the fucking
night
And I can't fuckin' sleep
And I'm up
And it's ridiculous
(Cuppa tea
Choccy bic
Obviously)
But it is
Just...
Not...
Acceptable!
It's...
So...
Fucking...
Annoying!!
I can't tell you!

I'M…
FUCKING…
FUCK!!!!!
I'M…
FED UP!!!!

Snookered – Frustration 2

Yesterday morning
Whilst
Sitting on the sofa
(For a change!)
I dropped
A tube of mouth ulcer gel
It slipped out of my hand
On to the floor
Went to pick it up
And it
Had disappeared
Gone
Nowhere to be seen
Vanished
Should have been there
On the floor
By the pouffe
(Or the poof
As I've always called them
Since I was a child)
But it was
Not
There
Mad
Bizarre
Completely ridiculous
And ludicrous
And absurd

Which brought to mind
The snooker analogy
'Getting the run of the balls'
As Neil Foulds often says:
Yer playing well
Red hot
Yer potting everything
You miss a pot
But the red
Bounces
Off the cush
Into another pocket
A fluke!
Them balls is going in off the chandelier
As they say
You cannot
Fuckin'
Miss!
No problem

However...
Yer playing badly
Yer can't pot a thing
Sadly
Yer go in off
Yer snooker yerself
Behind the yellow
You break up the pack
And leave
Nothing
Not
A single red
Is potable
And then
You
Miss
The final black
Off the spot
To lose the frame
And match

That tube
Of mouth ulcer gel
Should have been there
By my foot
With the furry paddle
On the floor
By the pouffe
Or poof
But it
Was not
It was not
There
That little tubey fucker...
Had
Disappeared

After Thought:

Dropped a steroid pill
On Saturday
Whilst standing
By the Sofa
On the green rug
That disappeared too!!
Quite pleased about that
There's something to be said
Fer the Bloomsbury Triangle!

Chemo Day 3

It's ten past five
It's cold
It's grey
It's Chemo day
Got me tea
Me choccy bic, obviously
Me cricket
On the telly
I'm okay
But...
It's Chemo day
Number 3
Will have a bath
In a bit
In the olden days
I'd 'ave 'ad a shit
Aaahh!
Memories...
Then multi coloured socks
Not paddles, not now
Green and black checked shirt
Red braces
Red cardy
A bit Tim Rice, Lloyd Webbery
Maybe, I know
But it works fer me
A squirt of me perfume
Issey Miyake, Nuit Dissey
For men
Have some brekker
Some pills
'Cos I'm ill
Then...
Off fer the stroll
See Scots Alex, en route

In Bloomsbury Square
Hello how are yer
I'm fine how are you
Where yer off to? He says
All in one breath
The butcher, I say
The butcher, okay
I do like to eat
But I don't like the meat
If yer know what I mean?
I'm off to Camden Town
Get some DVDs
Get 'em fer a pound
How's the cancer? He says
Not favourite, I say
Saw a great film
Billy Connolly
Not a good actor
Just plays himself
But he's good!
Bring you some solace
In your times of trouble, he says

So...to the butcher
Shoulder of lamb
Chicken wings
Belly of pork
Gonna cure some bacon
Gonna walk
That sarny walk
And...
Make some pork scratchin's
Smashin'
Bit of a fave
Wif the daughts

Twice round
Russell Square
See who's there

Maybe Pineapple Bark Man
Gok on the jog
(I'm a fan!)
A quick little sit
On Tricia's bench
(Not as fit
As I was)
Then back to the palace
Plant them tulip bulbs
That
Daught's friend Mia
Gave me
(They're a tad smelly
I have to say)

But I'm keepin' busy
That's the main thing
It's the only way
'Cos...
It's fuckin' Chemo day

5TH MARCH 2021:
Chemo 3...2

At the Macmillan Centre
Now
In the comfy
chair
All dripped up
(And nowhere to go)
Lovely nurse Marie
Just sorted
A cuppa tea
(No choccy bic, sadly)
Had to
Make do

With custard creams
But there were three!
Lady over there
Is weeping
Don't know why
Got a fair old idea tho'
Blue nurses scurry
A controlled hurry
Place is heaving
As ever
Time for the paper
Top horse trainer, Gordon Elliot
Is in the shit
Snapped
Having a sit
On a dead horse
Nay! Not a good idea
Seems to have posed
On the phone
For it
Astride the dead
Thoroughbred
Stupid, cocky, dick'ead
Shocking
Grotesque
Time fer a wee
Have to take my drip with me
On it's trolley
Awkward
Has a dodgy wheel
(Well...
It would 'ave, wouldn't it!?)
And back...
Moving on...
To the obit column
In the Daily Telegraph
A newspaper
I would not normally
Be seen dead with

(Not funny in a cancer centre!)
Our great local watercolour artist
Albany Wiseman
Our neighbour and special friend
For over 40 years
Has left us
Should be a swillin'
A glass or several
In his honour
This eve
But I'm completely off the sauce!!
Fuck!
I don't know
Very very concerning
Fucking Chemo!
A cuppa tea
Just ain't the same
Breakin' news...
From a passing nurse
Paul Gasgoine
The wayward troubled genius
Of English football
Is about to join
The Italian version of *I'm a Celebrity!*
Unbelievable
You could not make it up
Shit!
Need another wee
And, of course
Me single minded
Drugs trolley
With its wonky wheel
Is refusing to cooperate
As we desperately
Negotiate
A route around
An oncoming bald man
Who is very very poorly
One gentle nudge, I feel

With a wobbly wheel
Could send him toppling
Nerve wrackin' stuff

Two hours have passed...
The Chemo drugs are all in
(So am I!)
Steroids are go!
The weekend pump
Is attached
Alongside
The swollen bump
Of my stoma
And Colostomy bag
(Hernia issues, by the way...
But that's fer another day!)
There's a fuck of a lot
Hanging around down there
Really
Have to concentrate
When I go to the lavatory

Say a huge thank you
To nurse Marie
Then off to see the shivering Gina
Outside
Not allowed in, you see
'Cos of Covid
Then...
She's there!
In the comfy chair
In reception
Nice security man
Saw her shiverin'
And let her in
Just wonderful
We have a much needed hug
Good man, I say, good man
Pleasure boss, he says
With a big happy grin

Off we go
Unsteady
Hand in hand
United
Pins and needles
Kickin' in
As I hit the cold air
Gloves on
We stagger
Arm in arm
Feelin'
Like shit on a stick
Hoping the sofa
Will meet me half way
But I've got Gina
What a woman eh?
Fuck!
So Soo beautiful
In every way
I'm very lucky

5TH MARCH 2021:
Caught Nappin'

Later that night
Time for bed
Need to rest the head
Long day
But, you know...I'm okay
Considering
Curtains closed
Lights off
Candles out
Innocently
Finished my pint of squash
A burst
Of steroid Chemo thirst

3 big gulps
That's better
Had been told
With the fresh Chemo
To be wary of the cold
Possible
Chronic pins and needles
In the fingers and toes
Numbing of the lips
And the nose
Cold on the chords
Croak in the voice
But my drink was cool
Not really cold
So I boldly swilled
Fool
In seconds...
My throat was tight
Hard to breathe
Thought choking to death
May well be on the cards
Gina rushed to the kitchen
Fortunately
I'd boiled the kettle
Already
For the bedtime cuppa tea
(And choccy bic, obviously)
I couldn't speak
Breathing was weak
Shit!!
Am I dying?
Stood there terrified
Rigid
Against the wall
In the hall
Gina thrust the tea
At me
Drink! she gently urged,
Drink!
It's not too hot

Drink!!
I drink
Sink it in one
All drank
Fuck!
Thanks darling, I croaked

Almost instantly
I was...
Fine
Alive
Hadn't choked to death
Which was
Very nice
Went in for the cuddle
With Gina
Thanks, I said
You saved my life
Dramatic Nob, she said
With that smile
Fucking hell eh?
Well...
There goes that cold beer
I was looking forward to
On my 70th Birthday

Cricket (Angry Poem)

It's shit
The cricket
England have hit
An all time low
Useless
Depressing
You can't play
The sweep shot!
Got to move yer feet
Got to get to the pitch
Of the ball
It's ridiculous
It's like schoolboy cricket
Cross batted slogs
With no control
It's taking it's toll...
On me!
I'm getting really upset
Havin' a swipe
'Cos yer frustrated
Can't see the type of spin!
You do this for a livin'
Fer fuck's sake!
You should see the fucking
Spin
It's your job!!
I'm barking
It's doing me in!
Must be the drugs eh?
Steroid hit, Chemo fix
I hope so
Can't cope with this shit
For the rest of my fucking life
Fuck!!
And as for the fucking language
Fuck!!

It's an affront, I know
Sorry!
And I've only just
Got out of bed!
Goodness me!!

Not on Tricia's Bench with Mary Cade

Not
On Tricia's bench
This morn
Some other fuckers
Are on it!
Thinking of
Insulting them
Or physically threatening them
In some way
But it's not really me
Not today
We are on
Doctor Jennifa Ayesha Miah's bench
Next door
A very nice bench
No offence
Don't get me wrong
But it's just not the same
The joyous Mary Cade
Passes by
With her giant trolley
Not yer conventional shopping trolley
Mary's trolley
It more resembles the trolley
Pablo, the Majestic Wine man
In his van
Does his booze run with

To Dan, our neighbour
Upstairs
Of a Friday
She comes over
Full of happiness
I comment on her trolley
It's a new gleaming one
She's very pleased with it
She eulogises about my poems
I eulogise about her
Such a wonderful positive lady
Ask about Jeremy
Her lovely hubby
He is very poorly
She appears to be on top of it
Coping
Full of love and humour
Quite extraordinary
With a wave and a smile
Mary is on her way
She made me feel great
Made Gina happy too
Very few people can do that
We spot
Tricia's bench
Is now free
Chilly
But we have five minutes
Just Gina and me
Perfect
Say hello
Peaceful
Just the job

Then...
It's time to go
It's fucking steroid time

It May be Shit!

The Chemo
Seems to have given me
A big Bic rush
I just can't stop writing...
And writing...
And then...writing
Loads more
(Given me a sore hand, actually)
It may be shit!
But there's a fuck of a lot of it!
I hope it isn't
Shit
Obviously
For
Your
Sake!

Lost it!

I lost my temper
With my youngest daught
Sophie
Today
Shocking
Said some horrid
Horrible things
She was putting me straight
On the way
I was treating Gina
Her mother
My wife
(Of...forever)

Bossy
Controlling
Telling her how
To do things
For the best
Particularly in the kitchen
I think I'm a very good cook
And know best!
Not nice
Soph has a point
Tho'...this time
I wasn't convinced
So...I lost it
In my opinion
I was being helpful
(Gina has trouble
With our shitty oven)
But still...
Soph had a point
Annoyingly
Gina would probably
Have coped
Perfectly well, or better
With the shitty oven
Without my help
And, of course
She's sooo wonderful
She was never going to say
I was a pain
In the fucking arse
So...
Soph did!!
And I lost it
Shocking
Unacceptable
Probably fuelled
By the Chemo
And the steroids
But not on
I apologised to Soph

She wasn't 'avin' it
Fair enough
I went to bed
To escape and rest

Before going
I made some pork scratchings
A favourite of Soph's
Planning
To offer them up
As a peace offering
Later
Fingers crossed
On that one
But I wont be holdin' me breath

Sorry Soph
I'm not a nasty arse
But...
I do have my moments!
I lost it

7TH MARCH 2021:
Attenborough on Telly

Lovely
David Attenborough
The very nice
Very wonderful
Very old
Very...
Everything
Person
On the telly
Tells us
In the whole of South America
An area the size of a football pitch

Is disappearing
Every 5 seconds
Shit!
And...
95% of Colombian forest
Has disappeared
In the last several years
To farming
I have to say
Puts my cancer
In perspective
In a way
Or something like that!

7TH MARCH 2021:
The Triangle

Could not
Find my glasses
This morning
Searched everywhere
In the bed
By the bed
Under the bed
On the floor
By the door
Chest of drawers
In the loo
Down the loo
Under the loo
The Bloomsbury Triangle
Again!
Going
Crazy
Again
Get a grip!
Breathe, breathe, breathe...

Time for a wash
Couldn't have a bath
With all my bags
Stood there
Had a splash
Badedas bubbles everywhere
And...
Yes!
Sherlock!
Brace yerself!
They were there
My glasses
On my face
Covered in soapy suds
Fucking hell!
Fucking steroids!

Later...
Heading for the squares...
For the morning stroll
Couldn't find my rucksack
Anywhere
Gina waiting patiently
By the door
Not the Triangle again
Too large. Surely!
Can't find my bloody rucksack. I said
Gina turned...
A sudden guffaw of laughter
Hysterical almost
What? I said
It's on yer back, she burbled
What is? I said
Your rucksack!! She cried
Howling, delicately
Tears in her eyes
Oh God!! I said, Sorry!
Don't apologise, she said, let's go
I had a puff
I had a blow

Ohh! bloody stupid steroids! I say
I know, she says, lovingly
Best to blame something, you see
And not
My own
Stupidity...
Obviously

The Rings

Finally
In Brunswick Square Gardens
With Gina
And my rucksack
(Still on my back)
Saw these two large rubber rings
Slung over
The branch
Of a giant plane tree
Looked like nooses, from afar
Preparation for a double hanging
The hang man
A hairy young bloke, standing by
Rigid, concentrated
No baying crowd fortunately
Eventually
After intently staring
At the rings
For a while
He heaved himself up
Like in the world gymnastics champs
On the telly
Then dropped to the ground
Exhausted
Gasping for air
Almost immediately

That was the end
Of his gold medal challenge
I thought
Come on...
I could have done better than that, surely
You know...
Even with the cancer
And the Chemo
Tosser

Dark Moment

Had a dark moment
Around half five this morning
About dying
Not good
Decided to watch some coarse fishing
On Eurosport
To take my mind off
The death
This carp didn't look too well
As he laid there
Gasping for air
On Alan the fisherman's lap
While Alan
Took
The hook
Out
Carpy swam off
Spluttering a little
But at least
The large fishy beast
Was alive
Got to be a plus eh!?

Looking Back

Been looking back
A lot, lately
The sort of thing you do
I suppose
When you think
You may not have
A lot of time left
I may well have
A lot of time left
(He said, hastily)
But I just don't know
Which is a concern
I suppose

It's half four
In the morning
Remembering back
To 1983
A few years ago now
I was playing Tarvic
The monster
In a very, very dark version
Of Frankenstein
By the great playwright
Stephen Lowe
You should know 'im
Special man
At Plymouth Theatre Royal
One morning
Near to opening
I was practising my makeup
I'd shaved my head
And made it up
To look like
Four quarters of battered skulls

That had been sewn together
From the corpses
Of the battlefields
Of the Napoleonic Wars
I then poured
Very hot liquid gelatine
Over my head
My skin glowed
I sat
Very still, eyes closed
While it cooled
And set
A strange feeling
Could hear the cast
Rehearsing, giggling
All festive
In the room below
Once set
I screwed up my face
The gelatine
Cracked
In various places
I rubbed earth
And stage blood
All over my head
And neck
Into the cracks
Showed the cast
They recoiled, horrified
Job done!
I was very pleased
But felt
Very peculiar
Encased
Not quite me
An eerie
Feeling
I cleaned up
Took me a while
In my fragile state

Went to join the cast
For lunch
They had disappeared
Still not quite feeling myself
I set off for our usual boozer
We always went to
The Jolly Farmer...
No one was there
Apart from
About five hundred drunken
Christmas office revellers
In cracker hats
I squeezed to the bar
Thinking
The team
Must be there
Somewhere
They weren't
One amusing drunk
Pointed at me
Bursting into the refrain
'Nuts, whole hazel nuts'
To the tune
Of the Harry Belafonte calypso classic
From an advert
I'd done
Some
Years before
For which I was always getting recognized
A bizarre claim
To fame
Half the pub joined in
With cries of
Sing it! Come on! Sing it!
I refrained
From the refrain
They all laughed
I don't think
I did
They wanted to buy me

Lots of drinks
I refused
But they bought me a pint
Anyway
Found a seat
In a corner
On a table
With five giggling girls
Barely able to speak
From excitement
More than happy
To share their Christmas party
With a television star
I was very angry
Could not believe
What
Was going on
Sipped my warm beer
Chewed long and hard
On my slightly stale
Turkey and cranberry sarnie
Trying to get things clear
Getting crosser
With every swallow
Took out my red jotter notebook
And decided to try and express
My feelings
In four very terse
Very short
Very bitter
Rhyming verse...s
I had never written a poem
Before
I didn't finish my beer
Refusing more
From the giggling young ladies
Determined to cheer me up
Along with half the pub
With more singing
It didn't work

I left
Nursing my very terse
Very bitter
Very short
Rhyming verses...s
I was in a dark place

I was early back
To the cold, empty, rehearsal room
Another actor arrived
Full of festive cheer
And festive beer
Where did you get to Bob? he said
I had to drink yer pint
He laughed
I didn't
Silence
Are you ok? he asked
No, I said
I'm not alright...
Mate
Great make up Bob, he said
Terrifying
Yes, I know, I said
The cast assembled
They could see
Oh too clearly
That I wasn't quite me
I want to read you something, I said
I read them my four
Very terse
Very short
Very bitter
Rhyming verse...s
They were shocked
Horrified
There were tears
No laughter
(Which I'm keen on
Normally)

It wasn't funny
They all thought they'd told me
Where they were going
They hadn't
(With generous hindsight
I could have been wrong)
At the time
I quite
Def–fin–nite–ly
Was not!

I left
Feeling a lot better

Frankenstein
Opened
A few days later
Just before Christmas
Punters thought it was going to be
A jolly festive romp
It wasn't
It was full on dark
My first entrance
Thro'
The audience
In The Drum studio theatre
Frightened the shit out of them
A lot of troubled people
Left at various points
Lots of banging of seats
With cries of outrage
The patter of angry feet
When Frankenstein's wife, Elizabeth
Appeared naked
In bed
With me
Covered in my fake blood
After I'd been stabbed

I was rather good
One of the best things I've done
I think
(Turned me to drink, obviously)
I've been writing my
Not always
Very terse
Very short
Very bitter
But often dark
Often funny
Rhyming
(Or not)
Verse...s
Ever since
And this is no exception
But this is a long one
I like a long one
Aahh! Memories...
And it always makes me feel
So much better

9TH MARCH 2021:
The Number 14

Another
Empty
Number 14 bus
Just passed by
Sneezing
Been out in the cold
For too long
Caught a chill
No one
Popping in

For a sit
A ride
To ring its bell
Don't have to go
All the way to Putney Heath
Round the block
Would do
Just so they knew
Someone cared

10TH MARCH 2021:
3.20 am

Woke up
This morning
I say morning...
Head was gently...screaming
Eyes were aching
Wet with pain
Thought I'd been asleep
Forever
It was almost
Unbearable
It was only...
Twenty past three
Wot!?
Twenty past three!!
I could not believe it!
How could that possibly be?
Three twenty!
Twenty minutes past three!
Kept looking
At the clock
In disbelief
Sat up
Light on
Too much

Light off
Feet on the floor
By the garden door
And darkness
Checked the clock
Once more
It was three twenty...one!
Three twenty-one!
The relief
At least
Time
Hadn't stopped
It was moving
Rather slowly, obviously
But it was moving
In the right direction
My poor
Head
Was resting
On my shoulder
Sort of
Lulled over, heavy
My eyes were closed
Clouded
I straightened it up
My head
Tried to breathe
And ease
The hurt
The creaking
In my neck
Sat on the bed
My feet were aching
As well
My feet!!
The balls of my fucking feet!
For some reason
Why were the balls of my feet aching?
Give us a break
My feet!!

It was all
Rather frightening
I didn't know
What was going on
With my stupid body
Seemed to sit there
For hours
Feeling unhuman
Like something was taking me over

At twenty to four
I stood up
Put on my dressing gown
Gathered the mugs
My book
The newspaper
My pills
'Cos I'm ill
My note pad
My green Bic
Put on my paddles
Went into the hall
Bouncing
Ever so very slightly
Off the wall
With my head
And my eyes
And my fucking feet
Didn't feel
Human
Like something was
Taking control
Of me
(As I think I said)

Collected
My Grandson's supper tray –
Battered squid
(I know the feeling!)
Chicken popcorn

Chicken what!?
His tray had made it
As far
As the chest of drawers!

And I slowly
Gradually
Climbed the stairs
Over loaded
But it concentrated
What was left
In my head
(Which has always
Been debatable)

I arrived
After my arduous climb
In the kitchen
Put a fabric plaster
On my finger
Which was throbbing
For some reason
Do not ask me why!
Kept thinking
Is this all going
To stop...
Suddenly?
Life, I mean
Shit!!

And
Then
I
Very
Very
Slowly
Made
A
Cup
Of

Tea
Got
A
Choccy bic, obviously
And
Went
And
Sat
On
The sofa

I'd made it
I was free
In a way
Lovely
Silence

Then
I heard
A bird?
No!
An empty number 14 bus!
Bit early
Maybe...I was dreaming
Maybe...the bus was full!
I couldn't see
Maybe...
A full number 14!!
What a treat that would be!
Tooo fucking much!
I had a chuckle
All
Very silly

Satsuma

Just sat
On a satsuma
On the sofa
What an oaf...a
(My dad loved that word
I was often a prize one)
Squirtin' satsuma juice
All over
The ivory coloured
Sofa
Curiously
Got no juice
On my arse
As I hit it
Full cheek, as it were
Dead centre
Thus splittin' the sides
Of the satsuma
And squirtidge
Going horizontally
Not vertically
All over
The fuckin' sofa
Oaf...a!
Had just settled for a rest
But no
Cover in the washin'
Soapy scrubbin'
Towel over the stain
In hope of the capillary action
When I sit down again
Later
Liftin' the remains
Of the stain
Thank God

For O level chemistry
Tricky start to the day
Though

The Pill

The mildly
Annoying
Gravel-voiced
Nick Robinson
(He had throat cancer, I think
So no offence meant)
On the Today programme
On Radio 4
This stormy morn
Tells us
There is now
A tiny camera
Posing as a pill
You can swallow
To discover
Bowel cancer –
Three centimetres long
(Your chokin'!)
Two pics every second
For five to eight hours
Brilliant
But selfishly
It's a bit fucking late...mate!
Only jokin'

Reunited

Came out of my flat
This wild morning
Excuse me!
Came the cry, immediately
From this little chap
Scuttling across the road
In a flat cap
Excuse me! he said
Are you Bob Goody?
I am, I said, Yes, I said
Right, right, right, he said
Bubblin' over
We did an advert together
Years ago
You played my dad
Did I? I said
PG Tips
New Lemon Tea, he said
Very excited
We were at this counter
You and me
Drinking this lemon tea
Oh, I remember, I said
Lying
And you were a kid? I said
I remember you now
Your face
Still lying
It was working, however
He was relaxing
Turning to Gina, he said
Gleefully
Bob played my dad
In an ad, for lemon tea
He was so pleased

So was I, actually
1987, he said
Shit, I said, 33 years ago
We smiled
I'm John, he said, work round the corner
Bob, I said
Going to shake his hand
Then remembering
I know, he said, giggling
Ah yes, of course, I said
We live here, I said, pointing
I know, he said
'Cos my mum dropped you off
After the shoot
All those years ago

It was good to see
My son again
After so long
All grown up
And I think
He was glad
To see his old dad
Said I'd buy him a pint in the summer
In the Tav
I'd love that, he said
And off he went to work
A happy lad

The Er Factor

Boris er Johnson
Our er Prime Minister
Has an er factor
He...er...says er
Before nearly every...er...word
He...er...
Utters
It is...er...
Along with...er...
Just about everything else
About him
Fucking...er...
A...nnoy-er-ing!

13TH MARCH 2021:
Nobby, And His Amazing Technicolor Dreamsocks

Gina
Gave me
These amazing
Multi-stripey socks
For Christmas
They are beautiful
Stripey
Colourful
They very quickly
Became
My favourite pair
Of socks
Of all time

Problem is
I can't wear them
They're very thin, you see
Not ideal
For my pins and needles thing
In
The cold

This morning
I found them
Again
Looking forlorn
Having been confined
To the bench
As it were
Since being pulled on
For the indoor
Boxing Day fixture
Where they dazzled
Scoring many
Happiness goals
And giggles
With the family

Had a sudden
Flash
Of genius
I can wear
Another plain pair
Of socks (what?)
Underneath
The stripey socks (amazing!)
Thus showing off
The stripey socks
In all their glory (incredible!)
On warm
Toasty
Feet

Without a pin
Or a needle
In sight
Quite
Brilliant
I'm so bloomin' happy

Writer's Block

Haven't written a poem
Yet
This morning
Nothing
Not a line
Not a rhyme
Not a word
Not a letter
Not even
A hyphen
Or a semi-colon
Zilch
Many a ditty
Would normally
Have poured out
Of my ever faithful Bic
By now
I mean...It's late
It's 6 o'clock
For God's sake!
Worrying
Must be
Writer's Block

15TH MARCH 2021:
Housework

Dusted down the Christmas cactus
Put the new tea towels in the drawer
Shoved a few plates
In the cupboard
Swept up the spilt cat food
On the floor
Time for a serious
Sit down
I think

15TH MARCH 2021:
Naomi

This
Young woman
Has made her home
In the recessed porch
Of the Covid-closed Ryman's
On Lamb's Conduit Street –
A concoction
Of filthy blankets, cardboard boxes
A beige duvet
That has long since
Stopped looking like
A beige duvet
And at the front of her home
Hangs an old
Sheet
And a multi dull coloured
Crocheted blanket
All filthy
Giving a sort of
Front entrance effect
And a less than minimal

Protection
From the harsh winter elements
A bright orange bucket
Sits, at the foot
Of her bed
Alongside a child's white chair
And a pair
Of walking boots
In surprisingly good nick

She has been there
For weeks
Often
Sitting up
Head bowed
So distressed
And totally out of it
When passing
I've never had cash
And felt
Guilty
Today, I remembered
I couldn't see her, at first
She was buried
Beneath
The concoction
Of blankety filth
Excuse me, I said, gently
She jerked up
Fear in her eyes
Terrified
Sorry, I said
Holding out a fiver
Fresh from the Hole-in-the-Wall
I was a bit tall, and hairy, and scary
Nervously, she took it
Thank you, she said
Very confused
Look after yerself, I said
Stupidly
That, quite obviously

Had not happened
In a long, long time
But I wasn't to be bowed
She stared at me, lost
Get yerself a hot drink, I said
She looked a little
Bemused
How could I come out with
This clichéd
Shit!
Bye, I said, embarrassed
Then I'm fairly sure
I said, look after yerself
Again!
She disappeared
Back
Under the filth

We walked home
Bothered
I had a rant
About how selfish
Uncaring fuckers
In this world
Just about everyone, that is
Don't give a shit
About anyone
Other than them-fucking-selves
And particularly
The homeless
Choosing to ignore them
'Cos they're drunken
Drug-ridden parasites
Who deserve to be...ignored
So fuck 'em

Made me feel a whole lot better
Gina agreed

But obviously thought
I was possibly
A tad
Over the top
As usual
Still, as I say
Today
I felt better
But still bothered

Daught Soph
Got me the number of Street Link
A homeless charity
I called them
Rant number 2!
They listened
Concerned, rather amazing
They will call
Camden Outreach, they said
And let me know
Thanks Leah, I said, yer wonderful
No problem, she said
Thanks for calling
Pleased I did that, I said
Well done Nob, said Gina
Good deed for the day Daddaay, said Soph
I beamed
Self-satisfied
And I got back
To my extremely
Comfortable
(Somewhat
Cancer-clobbered, obviously)
Warm and cosy
Very well-fed
Middle class
Fucking life

Chemo Cocktail

2ml mouth ulcer gel
1 cube ulcer pastille
1 400mg Ibuprofen
1 500mg Paracetamol
Every 4 hours
20ml lukewarm salted water
With just a dash
Of Angostura bitters

The perfect cocktail
To accompany
The Chemotherapy
And the double cancer
With a mozzarella salad
On the side

Refreshing
However
Nice as that may sound
If I'm honest
Call me old fashioned
I'd prefer
A large Vod and Ton
And a bag of nuts

Naomi 2

Popped by
To see
The Ryman's lady
This morning
She was sitting up
There were
2 doughnuts
Sat on a grubby paper plate
Next to the bright orange bucket
She saw us coming
Hi, she said
Sort of smiling
With her mouth closed
Hello, I said
How are you? she said
Oh, we're fine, I said
How are you?
Yeah, I'm fine, she said
Are you? I said
Yeah, well, yer know
You just got to get on with it, haven't you? She said
I wasn't sure what to say
What's your name, I said
Naomi, she said
Sorry?, I said
Even my hearing is fucked now
Naomi, she said, slowly
Hello Naomi, I said
I'm Bob
And this is Gina
A little bit as if
I was talking to a child
Hello Naomi, said Gina
We're going shopping, I said
Do you want anything?

Ridiculous question
No, I'm ok thanks, she said
I held her sleep-troubled eyes
For a moment
Back in a minute, I said
Another nod
Another closed-mouth smile

We went to
The People's Supermarket
Next door
Got low fat natural yoghurt, fennel
A huge bunch of corian...dar
Naciente, pinot noir
The essentials

Back with Naomi
The doughnuts
Were still sat there
By the bright orange bucket
Looking rather sad
There you go, I said
Handing her a fiver
(Not as fresh
As the previous one)
And I didn't say
Get yerself
A nice hot drink
Thank you, she said
Smiling
Her teeth just
Poking thro'
See yer soon, I said
Bye, she said
Bye Naomi, said Gina

I hadn't mentioned
The call I'd made
To Street Link

I don't know why...
Well, I do...
Felt like
A betrayal in a way
As if we were
Poking our noses
Into her own
Private little world
However hellish that might be
Without being asked

We walked home
Up Great Ormond Street
Very quietly
Upsetting, eh? I said
Yes, said Gina
It's good you called that charity tho', she said
Reading my mind
Do you think? I said
Yes of course, she said
She may get some help
It's awful isn't it? I said
She could be dead
In a couple of years
And no one would fucking well know

We arrived home
Bumped into
Our lovely neighbour, Phillip
And his sister
And his whippet
On the street
Talked cancer
For a bit
Had a laugh
Then, after admiring
My slowly springing
Window boxes
We went in

For a sit
A cuppa
But no choccy bic, sadly
My mouth was too bloody sore
From the fucking mouth ulcers
From the fucking Chemo
I was feeling good
Though

16TH MARCH 2021:
Smashed it (Cabineted?)

I smashed
My head
Into the bathroom cabinet
Last night
Whilst bending over
To have a
Spit
(Not a shit!
Don't do that no more)
When brushing my teeth
Very very gently
In my poorly ulcer-ridden mouth
I must have
Brushed my teeth
Thousands and thousands of times
In this particular bathroom
To be more precise
Twenty-one thousand, approximately
(Just did the sum)
Since
My brother and I
Put that
Rather attractive

Stained beechwood
Cabinet
(Not a snip!)
On the wall
About 30 years ago
And I have
Never
Ever
Smashed my head
On it
When having
A spit!
Didn't just
Glance off
A corner
Or the edge of
The bottom draw
I smashed straight into it
As if
It wasn't there
Very nearly knocked myself out
Have a bump
On my skull
The size
Of a small
Basketball
To prove it
I know
I keep saying this
I know
But
What the fuck
Is going on?
At least it took me mind
Off me ulcers

It's Not A Joke Anymore

Things are continuing
To keep
Disappearing on me
Then reappearing
Blindingly
In the most obvious
Places
In plain sight
To anyone
Who has eyes
Why oh why
Is this happening to me?
Seriously
Am I losing it?
Got soo upset
Last night
When my bloody
Mouth ulcer gel
(An old foe)
Turned up
On my bedside table
After I'd scoured
The lounge
The kitchen
The loo
The bedroom
For a good
Half hour
Getting more and more
Anxious and upset
What are you doing? Enquired Gina
Sat in bed
With her tea
And choccy bic, obviously
Sorry darling, I said
Almost in tears

I can't find my
Bleedin' fuckin' arsin'...
Bloody...
...Losing my memory
At this point!
Mouth gel? Said Gina
Yes! I barked
Yes!
It's fuckin'
Disappeared
Again!!
It's there, she said, pointing
Where? I said
There, she said
Next to your phone
You brought it down, did you?
With the tea
And the books and stuff? I said
No, she said, you did
About half an hour ago
I didn't! I said
You did, she said
Gently
Seeing me slowly
Breaking up
But that's impossible
It can't be, I said
Why, why is this
Happening to me?
Why, I don't understand
How can that be?
Gina sipped her tea
Dunked her biccy
Too nervous
To say anything
Fearing
My total meltdown
Was imminent
I can't carry on like this, I said
I have to be

Going crazy
I went on
In the same vein
For a while
Gina
(What a woman!)
Trying to help me thro'
As I dissolved
Into a puddle
Of hopelessness
Wanting
To have a good cry
But, as ever
It wouldn't 'appen
I tried to read
I tried to make sense of it all
I tried to listen to Gina
I apologised to Gina
Don't apologise, she said
You're just
Not very well

Finally
Before the little tubey fucker
Buggered off again
I put some mouth ulcer gel
On my lips
And inner cheeks
And tried
With little success
To go
To sleep
Fuckin' 'ell

Apparently

Apparently
According
To many
Top jabologists
Around the world
The AstraZeneca vaccine
Is seriously
Dodgy
And in many countries
The vaccine
Has been
Withdrawn and flushed
Down the ol' lavola
However
Doctor Boris
Our very own
Jabologist's
Jabologist
Came on telly yesterday –
Looking
Very much like
If you
Turned him
Upside down
And dunked him
In a bucket of Flash
He could reach
Those corners
That other detergents
Can't reach
Where all the
Filthy shit
Gathers –
To tell us
All the world's experts
Are in fact

Wrong
What the fuck do they know?
The AstraZeneca vaccine
Is completely and utterly
Marvellous
And safe and wonderful
As houses
And we should all
Get an armful
(Which isn't 'armful!)
As soon as poss

My wife and daught
Have had
Their first armful
Of the AstraZeneca vaccine
And totally trust
Believe
Believe in
Adore
And worship
At the wordy er...altar
Of the mighty Doctor Flash
So if they get
Severe blood clots
And kick the bucket
As it were
It won't bother them
In any way
Or indeed
Myself
'Cos they know
As indeed I know
These world experts –
Top jabbers all –
To a man stroke woman
Are talking
A complete and utter load of bollocks

Wonder

Unfortunately
I turned on
Breakfast telly
This chilly morn
To see
The country music
Giant
Dolly Parton
Having
Her jab
All the while
Singing...
Vaccine vaccine vaccine vacc-see-ee-een
To the tune
Of her worldwide smash
Jolene

We then moved on
To our very own
Delightful
Sweet, petite
Superstar
Elaine Paige
Having her jab
And giving
Her smash hit song
Memories
From Cats
Very much the same
Vaccine treatment
As follows:
Vaccine, I'm having my vaccine
To protect against Covid
Make sure you have yours too

When you have it
You understand what happiness is
Look, a new life
Will begin

The sweet and charming
Breakfast telly presenters
Were beside themselves
With starstruck admiration
Awe
And wonder

Personally
I wanted
To throw up

18TH MARCH 2021:
Memories

In Mecklenburgh Square
Later
Saw this very old
Faded red
Volkswagen Beetle
With a registration letter A
A beautiful thing
Took me back to 1963
My first year
After failing my 11+
At Patcham Secondary School
The roughest school in Brighton
The Headmaster, Mr Budleigh
Permanently, stank
Of whiskey
(How did I know it was whiskey?)
And two school bullies

Palto and Gurney
(Names I will never forget)
Would, on a daily basis
Gather me
And my friends
In the playground
And hit us
With a wooden ruler
Rub chalk
On the playground wall
Followed by
Our arses
And...
If you were the chosen one
Have your head
Flushed down the loo
Aahh!
The good old days

P.S.
Many years later
When I had grown up
And Palto hadn't
I bumped into him
In the fruit and veg
In Waitrose
On the Western Road
And I chose
To punch him
On the nose...
But I couldn't do it
Sadly
I've never told anyone that before!

The Loaf

Just back
Drugged up, obviously
From Chemo 4
And in need
Of serious solids
A good feed!
No bread, sadly
Shit!
Not even a bit
Of mouldy old crust
I start to gibber
Then...
Thro' the Chemo steroidal mist
I see it...
The Hippy loaf!
A gift from
Daught Soph's
Friend
Mia the Baker
Wonderful
Five minutes later
I'm in heaven
Munchin' on
A corned beef, tomato and spring onion
Sarny
With just a hint of chilli
Yum!!
I now have a very very happy
Tum!!
Thank you Mia

19TH MARCH 2021:
Chemo 4 Day

Just had
Quite
A bad
Stabbin' pain
Behind my
Right eye
Does
This mean
I'm going
Blind...
As well?
Fuckin' 'ell

I've got the garden cane
Now where is that can
Of Dulux White Eggshell?

20TH MARCH 2021:
Feelin' Good

It's Saturday
5.20am
Again
Them Chemodrugs
Are pumpin'
From the bag
Around my waist
I'm up
Kettle on
Tea in pot
Biccy poised
Pills poised

'Cos I'm ill
I'm feeling...
Not bad, actually
Considering
Have a sip
Of warm saline
For my fast retreating ulcers
Not cold
Warm
Keen to avoid
Chokage, obviously
I swill the saline
As if tasting
A fine Rioja (if only)
And spit
Almost immediately
I feel my jaw
Clamping, locking
Really shocking
But the saline was warm! I say
Or would have said
Were talking an option
I swiftly
Pour my tea
And try to
Sip
It's really hot
Really sweet
I'm really scared
Will it make me worse?
Tea is dribbling
From my lips
(My mouth won't move!)

Thankfully
My jaw
Starts to ease
Instantly

And I begin to breathe
More happily
Mop up
My dribblage
From my soggy beard
And chest
And head fer that
Sofa
Shit!!
What a pratt eh?
But the saline was warm! I say
(Which I can say now!)

My grandson Zack
Comes in
Starvin'
After a nights gamin'
With his mates
D'ya want a pizza, I say
A pizza? He says, excited
Checking the time
Is that alright?
Well, I say
It's like supper really, you know
Isn't it, for you?
Oh yeah! He says, relieved
Beaming
Okay then, he says, don't mind if do!
We laugh
I put the oven on...

15mins later
It's 5.52am, approximately
With a happy Zack
Tuckin' in
To his Stone Baked Smoky BBQ Chicken pizza
In his bedroom

I'm on that sofa
Reflecting...
Bic in hand
On a surprisingly busy morn
You know...
I really was
Not ready for that
(It was warm!)
Not at dawn
With a warm saline
(Sorry to go on
But it WAS warm!!)

I'll tell yer what tho'
That warm choccy bic
Tasted better
Than ever
Don't yer know

21ST MARCH 2021:
Waking

When I awake
From a very deep
Afternoon sleep
On the sofa
I often feel
Very fragile
Very old
Very cold
Very lost
And a little frightened
I know...now
Those feelings
Will go
Once I'm on the move
Once I start to busy
But I'm not sure

They go
Very far
I think they
May
Hide away
Behind a happy place
And a bit like
Grandmother's Footsteps
When I was a wink
Ready to creep up
And tap me on the shoulder
And surprise me
Next time
I drop
My guard
And drop
Off

22ND MARCH 2021:
Surprise

The shit
In my colostomy bag
Is like bullets
At the mo'
And I've just spotted
This large spot
Where my arse
Used to be
Which I obviously
Can't see
With my eyes
And then...
There's this
Dried blood on my thighs...
Every morning
A new
Surprise

Anniversary 2

A year ago today
The lock down
Began
A year ago today
My cancer
Began
Again
And
A year ago today
I began
The Fucking Scary Virus Diaries
And the begans
Ran and ran...
And fucking ran!
And are still going strong
One year on

It's tragic
The death
The destruction
Of health
Is insane

But I have to say
Me good old faithful Bic
Is still going
And certainly
Won't complain!

One Year...

THE FUCKING SCARY VIRUS (CHEMO) DIARIES
...AND ON IT GOES...!

The Fly

There's
A fly
Swimming
In my mug
Of Earl Grey tea
The Oasis baths
On High Holborn
Re-opens on Monday
Thought he might
Have waited

So Tired

I was so tired
I had to sit down
Before
I blew my nose
When I rose
I couldn't remember
What I was
About to do
Before I blew
Have a Weetabix?
Make a cup of tea
For Gina? (plus choccy bic, obviously)
Water the plants?
Clean the windowsill, perhaps?
Take some pills
'Cos I'm ill?
I plumped for pills
('Cos I'm ill)
Seemed like
The safest bet, you see

A short while later
Gina appeared
From the bedroom
Morning darling, I said
Swallowing
A handful of cures
Morning Nobby, she said
I thought you were making me
A nice cup of tea
She said
Very gently

Cross

Got really cross
This glorious spring morn
I could not get
My fucking paracetamol
Out of the box
'Cos the bleedin' bloody blister strip
Got jammed
In amongst
The vast tome of instructions
When to take
Why to take
How to take –
Via the mouth, apparently
That's good to know
Been shovin' em
Up me arse
For years now
I've got a headache
For fuck's sake!
I don't need, to read
War and Paracetamol
To solve the problem

Assault

Woke up
At half 5
Nothing new there
(Bit of a lie in, in fact!)
Feeling like shit
Nothing new there, either
Bumped into the chair
At the end of the bed
Head butted the door
Not sure why
Maybe, it had upset me earlier
Tripped over a toy mouse
On the floor in the hall
Jammed my fingers
In the banisters
On the stairs
Fell up the final step
And sent the cat's water
Skimming across the kitchen floor
Just for good measure
For a man approaching 70
On an early morning assault course
I'd say
The boy done good
Wouldn't you?

Zack

My grandson Zack
A lovely innocent young man
Wrestling with finding
His way
Beyond delivery driving
And the PlayStation
Finds it hard to grasp
That I'm taking masses of drugs
To make me better
When, in his eyes
(And
In mine!)
They are making me
Very ill
Gina tried to explain
The wonders of Chemo
In vain
He wasn't 'avin' it
Stop taking them man! He said
Then I really will
Get ill, I replied
He swept his hair
From his eyes
Bewildered

Zack returned
To the sanctuary
Of his bedroom
And his tablet
And his phone
And his PlayStation
To ponder
This very strange world

Chemo 5

It's Chemo 5 day
Today
Sun is rising
In a clear blue sky
As I water
My chilli seedlings
My thyme
And the basil
They look so well
So green
They've been cherished
I am pleased
But...
Nervous
Of the day ahead
I've been feeling
Shitty
For a while now
And I'm not sure how
More Chemo
Is going to improve
The situation
Not in the short term, anyway

At the Macmillan Centre
Now
Awaiting infusion number 5
Place is heaving
The pre Easter rush
(Like the January sales, I suppose)
Sitting at a huge table
With many chairs
A very old
Very ill lady
Her over cheerful daught
And me

Another lady
In a grey turban affair
(And possibly no hair)
With her dinner tray
Containing
A disgusting looking bowl
Of...something
Yellow-ish
And...possibly a yoghurt
Has just sat down
Next to me!
Like...next to me!
Like...normal!!
Saw her moving towards
The chair
To my left
Out of the corner of my eye
(Odd expression that!)
Thought she was
About to move it
Or re-arrange it
Not...fucking sit on it!
Astonishing
Can't quite believe it
She is closer to me
Than I have been
To a human being (apart from Gina, obviously)
In over a year!
In a fucking cancer centre
There's an irony there
Somewhere
Made me very uncomfortable
Very strange
Excuse me, she said
Spreading herself out
Brushing aside my Guardian
Making room for her
Vomit like mush
Would you mind moving? she said
A pause

I'm sorry? I said
Puzzled
Can't have heard
Them words right
Would you mind moving? She repeated
More firmly
As if addressing
A deaf imbecile
To the next chair, she said
Pointing
Just there!
I looked at the chair
Then looked at her
In disbelief
But you sat down
Next to me, I said
You should be the one to move
Surely
No, no, no, she said
Pointing
Again
Those two there
(The very old lady
And her over cheerful daught)
Are chatting and laughing
And I wanted to read my book
Undisturbed
While having my lunch
Oh, I see, I said
Got you
She fixed her eyes
On me
Her bowl of...something
Was getting cold
Or maybe, warming up
It was hard to tell
I am rarely
Without words
But on this occasion
She had me

By the short and curlies
Just move up one! she said
Almost losing her patience
With me, this stupid idiot old man
No, I said
I'm moving to a comfy chair
One had, thankfully
Become spare
Over there, I said
(My turn to get pointy)
Oh goodness! She exclaimed
You really don't have to do that
Oh really! I said, I think I do!
Grimacing
Behind my mask
Thank you, she said
I headed for
The comfy chair
And, you know
I really don't think
She, of the grey turban
And possibly no hair
Was
In any way
Aware
There
Had been
A problem

Hot and Cross

Have just paid (in advance)
Twenty-three pounds 10p
For six hot cross buns
I know
It's not a typo!
Twenty-three fucking pounds and 10p!
From a fancy baker's
Waitrose's fancy
Hot cross buns
Are one pound sixty-five pence
For 6!
Even Heston Bloomin' annoyin's
Fancy hot cross buns
Are one pound eighty-five for 2
But Fortitude Baker's
(In The Colonnade
Opposite the closed Bird in Hand)
Hot cross buns
Are twenty-three pounds and 10 pence for 6
They'd better be
Large
And they'd better be
Fucking fancy
(Maybe
A solid gold cross!)
In order
To wipe this expression
Off my face...
Watch this space...

Poem for Jon

My great mate
The slightly dour
Slightly brilliant
Film director
Jon Sanders
Is...
I fool you not!
70...something today
I'm not being
Delicate here
(Not really me)
I just don't know
How old he be!
Having a guess
Seems inappropriate
Would love to
Have splashed out
On a large tomato juice (his tipple)
Or several
At the Golden Eagle
Marylebone Lane
In celebration
But it's not to be
Sadly
There's this fucking virus, you see
Did you know?
So...(that word!)
It's just...
Happy Birthday Jon
'Ave a great one, my son
And...
Go easy on the tabasco!
I love you mate

Good Friday

Up
Soon after 5
As usual
Good Friday
An exaggeration
Wasn't favourite, I feel
For Jesus either (as I recall)
I am just in time
For the Shipping Forecast
Dogger, Fisher, German Bight
North Utsera, South Utsera
The something Light Vessel
And all that
Very comforting
I do find it useful
Particularly
Being Fish Friday
Gives me some idea
How battered
My haddock might be

2ND APRIL 2021:
Hot and Cross 2: The Verdict

Just collected
The hot cross buns
From Fortitude Baker's
Well...
They are large
They have a cross
(Me too!
Not a solid gold one)

They have none
Of the traditional
Fruity yum –
Candied peel and cinnamon (mun)
More a cloying custard
And a dry...bun!
Really
Tasteless
Disappointing
Waitrose
Here I come!

7TH APRIL 2021:
The Beauty at One

Our darling granddaughter
Dolores
Is one today
One year on, obviously
From when
Beautiful midwife Jonny (her dad)
Delivered her
All on his own
While on the phone
To a medic
Talking him thro'
The basics
Of baby delivering
A step up (or two!)
From the paper round
Of his youth
It has to be said
Remarkable
And now the Beauty
Dolores
And her beautiful sister Constance

And her beautiful mother Seonaid
And her beautiful father Jonny
Will be with us
In chilly Bedford Square
On her first birthday
Could we be in
For that first cuddle...?
That first dribble on the shoulder?
That first game of peek-a-boo?
But is it safe...?
Is it allowed...?

Sadly...
It didn't happen
I couldn't get
Off the sofa
Let alone
Stroll to Bedford Square
Fucking Chemo

Praying

Nearly
Found myself praying
Today
Things were that bad
I was on my knees
Over the toilet bowl
Draining my colostomy bag
(I won't go into detail)
Suffice to say
It weren't pleasant
And I thought
Here I am
In position, in a way
Towel under me knees
Could double as a prayer mat
Haven't prayed
In decades –

Sunday school
In the Cub Scouts
My parents were
Staunch atheists
Yet, my Dad, the old fool
(As my Mum often called him)
Insisted I go
Confusing
Remember standing outside the church
Freezing
While our over jolly scoutmaster
Bill Somebody
Tried to cheer me
Do you know
What the bells are saying to us Robert, he said
No, I said
And he burst into song –

Come to church
Come to church
A quite brilliant
Inspired lyric, I thought
As I escaped to my
Favourite gravestone
Behind the church
Shivering
Till the end of the service

And now I found myself
On my knees
In front of the toilet bowl
A desperate man
Too weak to get up
Thinking
May as well give it a go
While I'm here
It can't get any worse
Apologise, you know
Say I've been...busy
And...
Would you consider
Taking on
A lapsed disciple –
You will remember
My Sunday school chortling
Hopefully
Spreading the Word
Of your good self!

A minor bag spillage
Brought me to my senses
My shit
For once
Had saved the day

Mr Philip

Mr Philip
Husband to Mrs Philip, obviously
Has just died
He was 99
A good innings, as they say
Like all world class cricketers
He's probably
Disappointed
The ton
Eluded him
Sadly
Unlike Stokesy, Rooty and Co.
He won't get
Another crack at it

10TH APRIL 2021:
13 – Chemo Blues

Laying in my bed
On the 13th floor
Gazing out
On a sun-drenched
London town
Glorious

Back in hospital
(Not so glorious)
Couldn't eat
Mouth raw with sore
Taste
Out the door
Hands and feet

Dry, achy, flaky
Not very usable
For the touching
And the walking
At present
Weight is
An issue
Heading towards
Zero
(Useful for
Space travel, I suppose)
Just attempted
A very, very small
Bowl of cornflakes
Tasted of grit
(Not that I've ever eaten grit!)
Bits of cornflake
Floating around
Then settling
On exposed
Tender
Nerve-jangling
Mouthy flesh
The following
Swallowing
A torture
Out of my window
Planes floating past
The Post Office tower
Are little comfort
Hoping to see
Gina later
She's coming to drop off
Some treats
I may be able
To eat
Celery juice
Sushi
Jelly and custard

A meal to savour

Just the thought
Of seeing Gina
And her beautiful smile
Her loving hug
Is so cheering
The reality
May just be
Totally
Overwhelming
But I'll give it a go

Ted

The 48 year old man
In the bed opposite
Is waiting for the results
Of a PET scan
He is understandably
In a terrible state
But trying to behave
Like he is waiting on
The result
Of a tight finish
In the 2.30 at Newmarket
Losing a tenner
Or losing a life –
If his brain has ceased to
Swell
Well...three months
More life
Is possible
However
If his brain has
Continued to
Swell
Well...couple of weeks
Max
He is trying to talk himself
With the help of wonderful Nurse Christine
Into the idea
That three months
More life
Would be brilliant
Time with the family
Holiday in Cornwall
Ice-cream, sandcastles
Fish 'n chips
In newspaper apparently

(Can you believe that Christine?)
And he can
Eat and drink his arse off
Without Maggie, his missus
Complaining
That he is killing himself
But she still
Probably will

12TH APRIL 2021:
Chemo Blues 2

Today
Is momentous
Opening day!
Had planned
To be
Outside the Tav, you see
My local
Salivating
Sat
At
A table
On an uncomfy chair
In the Museum Street gutter
The stench of drains
Driftin 'on the breeze
Awaiting delivery of that
Glorious, joy-filled
Crystal clear
(With elegant
Surface bubbles)
First pint –
London Pride
Abbot
Or both...at once!

But...no
I'm still on Ward 13
Nothing more
Need be said
Really

70

I'm 70 today
70!
Shit!
Wasn't ready for it
Not that well
For it, either
But at least
I'm home, in the bosom
As it were
I feel old...today
60 was...
Better
Had a big bash
50 was...2001!
Spaced out?
I don't remember
40 was...
All them years
Without a beer
And then it all began
30 was...
Married to Gina
Two small babs
Gemma and Seonaid
Another one to go!
The actin' was happenin'
Big time!
Whoa! Steady my son

Stay in touch
20 was...
Wild and boozy
Had my first taste of theatre
The operating kind
Unfortunately
Theatre technician, I was
Sussex County Hospital
Saw it all
From jam jars up the arse
(I sat on it! He said)
To kidney transplants
An eye opener, high drama
Then I went to RADA...
10 was...
Difficult
Mr Geerts
My rather unpleasant sports teacher
Dropped me
From the school cricket team
I was a very good opening batsman
In the Boycott mould
Told me I was useless, too slow
My dream, shattered
Not great
For the confidence
A year later
I failed my 11+
Huge fuss
In despair
I was meant to pass
0 was...
Nought!
Well...you have to start there
So I did
Mum and Dad
Were very happy with me
At that point

Now I'm 70!
With cancer (times 2!)
Don't like the war analogies
With a killer disease –
Fighting the fight
Losing the battle
Not good
Too much war
That's for sure
Prefer the idea
Of a race
10,000 metres perhaps
A long one
(I do like a long one!)
I'm off the pace, at the mo, obviously
At the back
Strugglin'
But I'm still there
Planning to work my way
One step at a time
(Sweet Jesus!)
Thro' the field
I may not win
But I guarantee
I will
Definitely
Finish

Another Beautiful Spring Day

Woke at 5
Yet again
Cold
Damp
Grey
And...
The weather
Was awful

The Kiss

The kiss
Was kind
Remarked Joe Johnson
On the snooker commentary
As the white ball
Made its way
(Having missed the blue)
To the baulk cushion
That was a kind kiss
He said again
Nearly a double kiss!

A kind kiss
A double kiss
Can't think
Of anything better
Nice one Joe

Results

Woke at 5
After a very dark night
No sunshine
Not even the occasional
Parting of the clouds
Had a dream
My life was
Being sucked away
By something
Not very nice!
(At least it wasn't cancer)
Not ideal
For starting the day
And what a day
You could say
It was PET scan results day!
Twelve more weeks of Chemo
Or twelve weeks of...sunshine

A phone appointment
At 3.45pm
With Dr Khan
Just 10 hours 45 minutes to go
Approximately
Time to kill
Took some pills
'Cos I'm ill
2 mins...sorted
No probs
Down to just
10 hours 43 mins now
Time just flying
429.6 recurring, similarly brief
But meaningful
Activities
Brought me to

3.45pm
Precisely
Relaxed
On edge
Calm
Anxious
The phone sat
Next to my old faithful
Bic
And choccy bic
A mug of Earl Grey
You might say
I was ready
For Dr Khan...

The phone
Did not ring
Not for the first time
Had a doc
Been late
On the clock
But this was
Unacceptable
An hour passed
Not very fast
(It took about sixty mins)
And the phone
Refused to ring
Even when threatened
With violence
At 5.15
I made a call
A stroppy receptionist
Of the brick wall variety
Answered
Telling me
Quite aggressively
My appointment
Was a face to face
At the Macmillan Centre

It was bollocks
And I pleasantly, as possible
Told him so
Back on the sofa
The silence
Continued...

16 hours later
(A troubled night's sleep
Under my belt)
Another call
No stroppy fella this time
Got matey, helpful Ella
The oncology PA
A different class
Of receptionist altogether
I inhale
And tell her my woeful tale
She shows concern
Encouraged to expand
On a roll
I suggest that senior docs
Don't actually give a fuck
About their patients'
Feelings
(As opposed to their ailings!)
Shit
An ugly quiet
Had I offended?
Of course I had
I was forced
Into an apology
The offended
Had become the offender

With a new appointment
For 1pm
Ella and I
Said a cool
Goodbye

Could I claim
A world record
For waiting time?
21 hours and 15 minutes approximately
Not bad
But probably
Not bad enough
My original nervousness
Had lost its lustre
But I tried
To muster up
Some fear and panic
Normally, not a problem
But normally
Has not been normal
For some while

I settled down
To the final 3½ hours –
Sofa
Cuppa
Choccy bic
And the very latest Val McDermid –
Still Life...

Mr Goody?
Ah! Dr Khan!
Sorry, for the late call, he said
(It was 1.15)
Just the 21½ hours doc, I said
Had a good book
So it wasn't a problem
The doc was confused
I explained, in some detail
He was still at a loss
I decided not to pursue
The matter
Any further
Unlike me
Anyway...

You have the scan results, I said
With surprising optimism
A beat
I have some wonderful news Mr Goody, he said
Another beat
The nodes have shrunk
The cancer is in remission...
For the time being, he said
So...
No more Chemo
For now, he said
We'll see how you're doing
In July
Wow!! I said
(Or Fuck! to non docs)
I looked up
To see across the room
Gina beam
She'd got the gist
A glorious sight to be seen
3
Months
Off!
No
Fucking
Chemo
I could be
Me
Again
Possibly
In a few weeks
Thank you doctor, I said
I am so happy
See you in July, he said
I could hear his smile

The hug that followed
With wonderful Gina
Was the greatest hug
Ever seen

In the world
No words
Just hug
And then...
A kiss
Bliss

2ND MAY 2021:
Sunday Morning

Saw this lady
Bright Yellow
Duvet type jacket
Huge dark glasses
Black mask
Out fer a jog
With her sausage dog
This chilly
Sunday morning
On the embankment
She was struggling
To keep up
With the little porkster
And paused fer breath
The wee chipolata
Was not having it
An argy-bargy ensued
Involving
A lot of yappin'
On both sides
Needless to say
The dog had his day
And the bright yellow duvet
Glasses
Slightly askew
Stumbled on

The Limp (Honesty)

Man
With a very comic
Limp
Walking down our street
At extreme pace
Almost trotting
Pain in his face
Pain in his feet
Or foot
I imagine
Slowing down
I'm sure, would help
And would gain
Some sympathy
At least
From me
And not
Unfortunate
Child like sniggering

Shocking, mocking
Best
Keep that
To meself

14TH MAY 2021:
My Head

Things
Seem to go
Into my head
These days
And not hang around

For too long
Sometimes
Only a couple of mins
Before
They're gone
I'm just hoping
It's
Forgetfulness
And not something else
More...
Sinister
Like...
Bugger!

Results 2 (Three months on)

I have rehearsed
In my mind
So many times
What I will do
What I will say
If the doc
Tells me today
The game is up
The ball
Is well and truly
On the roof
And I will soon be
As was the legendary parrot
No more
Will I say
That's okay
I'll deal with it
Or will I say
Fucking hell!

I don't want to die
(But then again
Who does?)
Or will I
Bemoan the fact
I don't have God
(The Almighty)
To turn to
Bit late in the day
To sign up
You might well say
He won't buy it!
Or will I just
Break down and cry
Bawl me eyes out
It's hard to know
But one thing
I won't do
As is often my wont
Is see the funny side
Because
Quite simply
Finally
There isn't one

Then again...
There might be!

Sorry to keep you waiting Mr Goody, said Doctor Khan
I'm getting used to it, I said
Smiling
Beneath my mask
We'd waited nearly 3 hours
Suzy, my colorectal nurse
Passed by
A couple of times
I raised a friendly palm
Hoping fer an update
She didn't see us

I'm easily missable
Doctor Khan glanced at his screen
I have some bad news, I'm afraid, he said
Ah! I said
The cancer has spread
Thought it might have, I said
Another glance
More nodes up the middle back, he said
Lesions in the lung
Nodes on the wall
Gina, squeezed my hand
The lung? I winced
It's containable, he said
Unlike the liver or the kidneys
Right, I said
How's the neuropathy?
Not good, I said
Tingling, numbness, swelling
I stumble a lot
With the occasional tumble
So...we'll go
For a different Chemo regime, he said –
Folfiri®
Sounds like a cocktail, I thought
(Ice and lemon?)
Which, I suppose, in way, it is!
For six months, he said
Shit, I said
He glanced up
You have a lovely head of hair, he said, smiling
Thanks, I said
You're going to lose that
Great, I said, it gets better
Another gentle squeeze, from Gina
There is also, he said, an extra drug
Not on the NHS, I'm sorry to say –
Avastin
You can talk to Mr Bridgewater next time, he said
I was having a job to take it all in

He handles the private side
A nod, too much
A look to Gina, quite lost
I'm sorry, he said
I shrugged
A screwing of the lips
A beat
How long have I got? I asked
Impossible to say, he said
Thanks, I said

We left
Had a hug
A pint, I think, I said
We smile
Holding hands
We headed for the Malborough
My old local
From RADA days
And a pint
And a half
Of Guinness
And a bag of nuts
Cheers!

18TH JULY 2021:
Some Days Later

Some days later
Now
On Tricia's bench
In Russell Square
Shaggy dog
Having a pee
On the tree
In front of me

And...well...
Still trying
To get to grips
With it all
Fuckin' 'ell!
New Chemo
New extra drug
If me pockets are deep enough
No fucking hair
Been working it out
Fortnightly infusions
For 6 fucking months!
Covid swab, blood tests,
Urine dipstick
(What!?)
On Christmas Day
Then...
Turkey drumstick
In one hand
Cracker
In the other
The final Chemo
On the 28th!

What can I say?
I'm okay
I'm dealing with it
And...
I'm still here

My Penis 2

Seeing Fiona
This morning
At UCH
Westmoreland street
About my ongoing
Erection issues
(See *My Penis,*
The Cancer Collection)
I've tried the pump
Not fer me
Involved
A lot of lubricant
And rubber rings
Not my thing
Messy
And pain
Not ideal for the passion
Sex
As I recall
Is meant to be fun
It's looking like
My only option
Is the dreaded
Erection injection
In 'The shaft'
Tho' don't want a repeat
Of the Wigmore Street
Debacle
(See *My Penis*
Again!)

Sitting
Opposite Fiona now
In a somewhat
Sterile, office like room

Full of Chemo
Full of steroids
And I don't somehow
Much fancy, I say
Sitting here
Shoving a hypodermic needle
Into 'The Shaft'
Of my wan and weary
Member
And seeing
If it will rise
To the occasion
(To my surprise!)
Before hitting Wigmore Street
I hope!
Can't cope
Fiona
Is with me, on this one
Understanding, caring and smiley
We agree
To meet post Chemo
In the new year
And give it a go
I say
Thank you
And add
Top of my bucket list
Is making love
To my beautiful wife Gina
Followed by
The Pyramids
We'll see what we can do, she says
With a big smile
We shake hands
I wish Fiona Happy Christmas
And leave
A happy man

The End

I think
We are coming
To the end
The worst
Of the virus
Could well be
Past us
And we're getting back
To something like
It was never like
Before
Can't say the same
Fer me cancers, obviously
Back on the fuckin' Chemo
As you know
With a new drug
Avastin
Ups me chances
Of Chemo success
By 20%!
(Or 5%
Depending what Doc you talk to!)
Impossible
For which I'm paying
1,937 pounds
A hit
I'm having 11!
To stave off
Heaven
A little longer
Bit
Of a shit
That
Boris
And the boys

Took it off
The freebie list
Survival of the richest
It would seem
But what can I do?
It has to be done
If the race
Is to be won
Or at least completed
Possibly
A little earlier
Than I had in mind
But never mind
(Good innings
And all that)
As I say
I'm dealing with it
Sort of...
It's not easy...

13TH AUGUST 2021:
Sunflower

My first
Sunflower
Came out
This morn
At 6 o'clock
In my window box
Tall
Lean
Yellow
And beautiful
Standing there
Swaying slightly
In the dawn summer breeze
Head bowed
Looking down on me
I grew you, I say
You're all mine...
Was that a smile?

BOB GOODY

Bob is an actor, writer and performance poet.

He trained at RADA in the early 70's and went on to work extensively on stage, telly and film. While at RADA he met Mel Smith and formed a partnership (Smith and Goody) based on laughter! They co-wrote and performed three black comedy musical plays, *'Ave you 'Eard The One About Joey Baker, Irony in Dorking,* and *The Gambler* (Hampstead Theatre, The Harold Pinter Theatre, West End), and the *Smith and Goody* television series.

Bob also co-wrote the BBC sitcom, *Wilderness Road* (with Richard Cottan), the libretto for the opera *The Fashion* (Oper am Rhein, Dusseldorf), and was co-adaptor (with Dan Jemmett) and performer of the Berlioz opera *Beatrice and Benedict* (Opera Comique, Paris) – being roundly booed on the opening night by the French punters for fiddling with their beloved Berlioz! A career highlight!

Bob began writing his verse after an incident whilst playing Frankenstein's Creature at the theatre Royal, Plymouth in the early 80's. (see *Looking Back p. 141.*) He performed his first poetry night in his local boozer, The Plough, in Bloomsbury, before hitting the poetry and comedy clubs, and then developing several stand up poetry shows, including *Mixing with the Sharks* and *The Bite of the Dog* (Edinburgh Festival, Soho Theatre West End and...beyond!). But always returning to his local for sweaty, rowdy nights with his great poet pal Andrew Cuthbert as The Bloomsbury Bards. Sadly, them poetic juices began to slow down a tad in recent years (apart from the occasional poetic gem, obviously).

Then...along came bowel cancer! And...his old faithful Bic (pen) took off, producing *The Cancer Collection*. A year later and the nation's health was under threat, and the Bic once more got scribbling, producing the epic *Fucking Scary Virus Diaries*.

Bob has been married to the beautiful Gina for ever, and has three beautiful daughters, Gemma, Seonaid and Sophie, and lives in sunny Bloomsbury.

9 781913 958251